Ridgemoor

A Novel Exploration of Agile Benefits and Blockers

Jeremy Worrell

Technics Publications

SEDONA, ARIZONA

115 Linda Vista, Sedona, AZ 86336 USA
https://www.TechnicsPub.com

Edited by Jamie Hoberman
Cover design by Lorena Molinari

First Printing 2024

Copyright © 2024 by Jeremy Worrell

ISBN, print ed.   9781634625692
ISBN, Kindle ed.   9781634625715
ISBN, PDF ed.   9781634625722

Library of Congress Control Number: 2024949293

Contents

Prologue

A common consultancy mantra runs as follows:

Tell them what you're going to tell them,
tell them, then tell them what you told them.

I'd rather not pre-empt, so won't attempt the first of those here. But I do feel the need to head-off possible misunderstandings— especially for international readers.

First, to steer clear of any suggestion that the novel borrows from the real world, I've chosen to set it in a sector in which I've never worked. My most recent exposure to university life was thirty years ago, and then only as a student. So, I hope readers will overlook any misrepresentations of contemporary higher education. These shouldn't distract from the underlying messages.

Second, readers should note that, while I have worked internationally, I'm from the United Kingdom. Rather than pretending to be something I'm not, and attempting to write in American or International English, I've stuck with British parlance and idiom. I hope everything is still intelligible to everyone as a result. If not, I'm confident that committed readers will happily resort to a dictionary.

Third comes a related note—after much deliberation I decided to adopt a hybrid of UK and US English. Most of the spelling and hyphenation follows UK standards, but I've made some exceptions where there seemed too much potential for confusion. In doing so, I of course run the risk of upsetting *everyone*. So please read kindly, remembering that I mean well.

Fourth, now you know that I'm British, and have chosen to write about higher education, you won't be surprised to find that the setting for the novel is an English university. This setting requires me to use two terms in ways which may be unfamiliar:

Faculty – the usual name for a single academic department or school within a UK university

Vice Chancellor – the most senior executive officer, comparable with a CEO (whereas the 'Chancellor' is a ceremonial role, often occupied by a prominent public figure)

Fifth, characters in the book occasionally use the term 'guys' in their dialogue. In each case, it refers to a group of people of unspecified gender. I consider this usage to be typical, hence its inclusion.

And finally, on the theme of gender, please note that one of the characters in this novel uses the pronouns 'them', 'they' and 'their'. I apologise for any confusion this may cause, but not for representing the contemporary workforce as best I can.

I hope you find the story that follows both elucidating and entertaining.

Cast of Characters

At Ridgemoor University

Carla – the university's Vice Chancellor

Penny – the Finance Director

Harri – the People Director

Vanessa – the Chief Digital & Information Officer

Pedro – the Chief IT Architect

Aisha – the Head of Information Security

Colin – the Head of IT Infrastructure & Operations

Sukhi – the Head of Digital Development

Tim, Jack – other senior developers, reporting to Sukhi

Olivia, Abhi, Bea and Charlie – product leaders in Student Services

Outside Ridgemoor

Maddie – Vanessa's school-age daughter

Yogi – Vanessa and Maddie's pet dog

Casey – an intriguing stranger

Week One

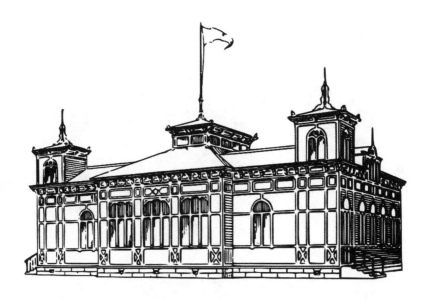

Monday

"That's not what I'm hearing!" Carla retorted sharply.

Although she prided herself on applying evidence and reason in every difficult discussion, she was losing patience. Her Chief Digital & IT Officer, Vanessa, persisted in defending the Digital team's speed and efficiency, but Carla just couldn't match that to what she was hearing elsewhere. And as Vice Chancellor of Ridgemoor University, Carla was ultimately accountable.

Nonetheless, she felt immediate regret for her overly forceful reaction. Since she joined Ridgemoor two years ago, she'd come to like and trust Vanessa, and in any case, could hardly provide any specific evidence of her own to help her understand the problem they now faced. Carla barely understood it herself. There simply wasn't the data.

"We've plenty of room for improvement, yes," Vanessa accepted. "But we've come so *far*! For one thing, we move much faster than we did two years ago … don't you agree?"

"I wish I could," Carla sighed, sitting back down at her desk, "but no one outside your team sees it that way."

Vanessa was taken aback, "I honestly don't see why not. Only last week, we released the latest version of *Syllabize* two weeks ahead of schedule, and this kind of thing happens regularly now."

Carla could see that Vanessa was genuinely perplexed.

"Sounds … useful. But nonetheless, the message isn't landing. Can you please find out why, and let me know how two views of the same team—*your* team—can be so strongly opposed?"

Vanessa paused, then accepted the inevitable. "I'd like to, yes. I'll investigate, and let you know what I find, next … month?"

"Sounds good. Start with Olivia. Let's talk again next week."

Leaving Carla's office Vanessa suddenly felt the aftershock of the attack. So, instead of walking straight back to her own office, she took a diversion past the *Coffee Shack*. This seemed like a double espresso-sized problem.

Carla hadn't stated *outright* that a month was too long to wait, but clearly indicated that she wanted fresh insight next week—and

Vanessa wasn't sure where to find it. This issue had come out of the blue, and she had yet to get any kind of grip on it.

She was uncomfortably unaccustomed to feeling frustrated with Carla, who usually seemed so grounded and reasonable. Since they first met a little over two years ago, it had seemed they had an understanding. They used similar verbal expressions, were both serious and succinct, and even shared many mannerisms.

Carla's proposed course of starting with Olivia, the outspoken Product Manager responsible for *Syllabize*, somehow made Vanessa nervous. She first wanted to canvass her own team to gather useful background information about the problems they saw, but emailed Olivia anyway—privately hoping for a delay in the other's response.

She'd start her internal investigations with Sukhi, her Head of Digital Development. This being Monday morning, they would likely be attending a series of "retrospectives"—meetings in which each development team examined its ways of working, seeking improvements. She could wait a few hours, so she asked Sukhi to join her straight after lunch.

In the meantime, Olivia had been disappointingly rapid to reply, suggesting a short breakfast meeting tomorrow. Taking a reluctant slurp of espresso, Vanessa accepted the invitation, thinking how important it would be to get what she could from Sukhi today, ahead of tackling Olivia.

"Come in!" Vanessa shouted through her open office door when Sukhi appeared. They were ten minutes late, but not to worry. Although she preferred punctuality, Vanessa was learning to live comfortably enough with the apparently inevitable modern malaise of everyone being a little late for everything.

"Grab a chair," she offered.

In response, Sukhi sat on the edge of an easy chair, looking anything but easy.

Vanessa decided to start with topics other than work.

"How's the gaming going?"

Although now in their thirties, Sukhi was still a fan of online role-play games. Their latest craze was a space-based game where Sukhi could team up with others online, fly missions, trade goods, save planets, and earn military stripes.

"Pretty good actually … when I have time to play," they lamented. "I just got promoted to Admiral."

"Maybe I should try it one day!" Vanessa suggested, mustering as much conviction as she could. "And how's everything in Digital?"

"Mmmmm. Okay, I guess," came the hesitant reply. "But the teams are getting more and more reluctant to improve."

Coincidence? Vanessa wasn't sure. But it gave her a great lead into the conversation. "I'd love to hear more. Your Digital teams are hugely important to the University, so it would be comforting to know that they're still firing on all cylinders."

"I don't know what the problem is yet … at least not exactly," replied Sukhi. "A couple of months ago, the *Syllabize* developers started postponing improvements that we'd agreed on in their retrospectives. But in the last two weeks, they've even stopped volunteering new ideas. It's really weird."

"Might someone in another team know what's going on?" Vanessa probed.

"Well, I asked around, but most people were pretty subdued on the subject. I didn't hear anything I could make any sense of."

"Interesting. I wonder what that means?" Vanessa thought aloud, then paused before continuing.

"Look Sukhi, I've just been with Carla. She's started questioning how effective we really are. I wasn't expecting this, given our successful transition to Agile a couple of years ago. I thought we had everything well-tuned now, and that our reputation was strong right around Ridgemoor."

"Me too!" Sukhi agreed, keenly. "We've done everything you're meant to. You know, defined our Digital products, connected with the Product Managers, built backlogs, allocated people into squads, and given them the right tools to work with. All my peers in other organisations are doing the same things."

"Right. Yes, I thought so. So do you get a lot of feedback from outside Digital?" Vanessa quizzed.

Sukhi shifted a little in their seat. Questions about other people's opinions tended to make them uncomfortable. It was pretty clear to Vanessa that they preferred questions about code and configuration.

"Erm. Not loads, no. Except when something goes wrong. Then everyone's pretty quick to jump in and tell us what they want."

"But I guess you must hear from the Product Managers regularly?" Vanessa checked, edging a little closer to Sukhi. She thought she spotted them shift away in response, almost imperceptibly, before answering.

"Not too often. But everything we do is in pursuit of their needs."

Something didn't fit. Sukhi and the team had one job: to develop what the Product Managers needed. But they weren't nurturing the relevant relationships, and meanwhile, it sounded like commitment might be waning inside Digital. She knew better than to pursue the point with Sukhi right now, but nonetheless, was sure to file it away mentally ahead of tomorrow's meeting with Olivia.

"Understood," was all she said in reply, and that seemed to satisfy Sukhi. "Any other concerns to raise?"

"No, nothing. Unless you'd like to translate our web app into Mandarin?" Sukhi grinned, happy to be talking technology again.

After cycling home that evening, Vanessa ran her daughter to the school's evening chess club. Maddie had started taking an interest in the game after a couple of her more influential peers started playing. Funny how hobbies can fall in and out of fashion so quickly, Vanessa thought. Maybe she was getting old?

As usual, Vanessa took a seat on the sidelines, and started the assault on her emails and chat messages.

Then, unusually, an unfamiliar drawl interrupted her concentration.

"I'm pretty sure I've seen you somewhere before. Are you a CIO?"

Startled, Vanessa turned to look at the source, sitting a few yards to her left. "Yes. Well, *CDIO* anyway. I do Digital too. Sorry, should I know you?"

"I don't think we've met. But I reckon I read your profile in last year's list of top CIOs. Vanessa … something, yes?"

"That was me! I'm flattered. I didn't think anyone actually read those things … erm …?"

"Casey. But don't laugh – I'm from California. And anyway, I didn't choose the name. So, you were responsible for that super-successful Agile transition, right?"

"That was the story. Though right now, I'm starting to wonder. Looking back, it all seemed to go like clockwork. We did all the stuff that the books and experts recommend, and we got plaudits from all sides. But just this week I've started getting weird feedback."

The corners of Casey's mouth twitched as he responded. "Sometimes borrowing all the best practices doesn't cut it," he postulated impenetrably.

"You seem oddly well-equipped for this conversation! Is this your area of interest, Casey?"

He smiled in a wistful, world-weary way, and embryonic wrinkles played around his eyes.

"You could say that," came his enigmatic reply.

"Well, any help would be much appreciated," she implored with real feeling. "I have loads of questions!"

"Let's chat about it next time we meet," Casey suggested to Vanessa's emphatic nods. "Sorry, I've got to go. But here's something to consider, how would you know if it *was* working well?"

He drifted out of the hall and into the dark of the evening, leaving Vanessa wearing a pensive, puzzled expression—her thoughts a million miles away from Maddie's momentous checkmate.

Monday's main messages

✓ *Respecting only the rituals of a new way of working won't be enough to create compelling change.*

✓ *Dialectics mean that people will take divergent views on the same phenomena, making dialogue crucial to change.*

✓ *Make sure you know what good would look like before trying to get there.*

Tuesday

They'd agreed to meet at the *Coffee Shack*. Far from inspiring, but it was convenient, and the very place that Vanessa would have started her day in any case. She arrived a little early, hoping to get her thoughts together before their discussion, but she had only just sat down when Olivia loomed into view.

The two smiled cordially, then passed the time of day for a few minutes. They'd met only twice before, and only in other company, so it would help to socialise a little before getting down to business. Maddie's chess success was the headline from Vanessa, while Olivia outlined her training plans ahead of an imminent triathlon.

"I don't know how you do it," Vanessa shared, somewhat reluctantly. "I already have to look in ten directions at once, without setting myself new challenges too!"

"I guess it's just prioritisation," Olivia replied in amusement. "I have to accept that other things will slide sometimes. And, of course, not having kids gives me a lot more time."

"Well, it's admirable all the same," Vanessa offered. "Look, I'd better get to the point before we miss our chance. I met Carla yesterday, and what she said made me want to get a better handle on how people really feel about Digital. Anything you could share?"

"I wondered if that might be the theme. Yes, I think I can help. My view is …," and Olivia paused to collect her thoughts before conceding, "they're a nice bunch, but they all seem to be stuck in their technology bubble, and pointing in the wrong direction!"

Vanessa was shocked and stumped. She had no idea how best to respond. "I'm listening. But I confess I'm surprised. Could you expand?"

"Of course. Look, it seemed really promising a couple of years ago. We were making all the changes that the experts prescribed, and there was an almost tangible enthusiasm from your teams. Then … I don't know what happened. It's almost as though by industrialising Agile we lost that engagement. That spark. We meet them less often now, the conversations are narrower and shallower, and they always talk about the *volume* of their work instead of its *value*."

Vanessa nodded automatically, subconsciously scrutinising Olivia's face in the hope of further clues. Ten seconds later, she realised she was still nodding silently, and that Olivia was now scrutinising her right back. She laughed in surprise, and luckily Olivia joined in.

"Seems like this is new news?" Olivia smiled. She hadn't expected to surprise anyone with what she said, let alone the respected CDIO.

"Honestly, yes."

"I wish I could tell you why it's happened," Olivia added. "I mean, they own the platform, right? Maybe they've just got bored?"

"Hold on, though," Vanessa prompted. "Doesn't your team own the platform, really? I mean, we have the technical skills, of course. But we work to your backlog of new features."

"Yes, true. But I wouldn't say we *own* the platform. We're just not equipped for that in Student Services. We know what we want, yes—at least, usually—but we don't have the faintest idea how to wrangle the technology to get it."

"I see. Yes, I suppose I know that really. But it feels like the boundary of responsibility isn't exactly where I'd imagined. This is really helpful, Olivia. Let me take it away and work it through some more."

As the two rose to leave the *Shack* and return to their offices, an afterthought came to Vanessa.

"Just one more question, what would it look like if this was all working well?"

"Wow. That's a tough one. Let me give *that* some thought! We'd better meet again soon."

"That's not what I'm seeing!" Aisha retorted sharply.

Tuesday was SLT day, when Vanessa's Senior Leadership Team— all of her direct reports—met to discuss matters arising. There always seemed to be more matters than time available to talk about them. Perhaps another example of Parkinson's Law in action, or just a consequence of people's instinct to talk more than they listen. In any case, things had improved since she'd rebalanced the team last year.

Aisha was Vanessa's knowledgeable Head of Information Security. Although that topic was low on the agenda this week, the team had drifted over to it in response to Sukhi's update on Digital development.

"I know you're not *ignoring* our security exposures," Aisha admitted. "But you're not fixing them either. I don't get it. Aren't the risks clear enough yet? The top two alone could irretrievably damage Ridgemoor's reputation."

Sukhi sighed. It was a familiar discussion, inside and outside the SLT forum. "Like I keep saying, we're stacked. We have a stream of *Syllabize* features to develop, which will keep us fully occupied for six more months. We can't conjure up more time. And I can't afford more people."

"But it's my responsibility to maintain security around here," Aisha complained. "And I can't do it without everyone's active collaboration."

"I know. I get it. I'd probably say the same if I were you. But I don't know what else to tell you!"

Vanessa intervened. "You're both right. Aisha, your team can't directly implement the fixes and safeguards you feel we need. And I don't want you to start hiring your own developers to do it. We can't have two development teams working on the same code in parallel! So the answer has to be with Sukhi."

She continued, "On the other hand, Sukhi, you don't see a way to free up capacity for the fixes. You *and* Aisha have tried to highlight the most pressing threats to Olivia and the others, and get corresponding mitigations on their backlogs, but without success. It's about time we tackled this problem, together, instead of allowing it to drift. If we don't, who will?"

She left the rhetorical question hanging, and paused to let its implications sink in.

"So do me a favour, would you?" Vanessa directed the two. "Could you each think up a few ways we could get out of this hole, while trying to minimise any adverse impacts on each other? Then we can discuss them as a team at the next SLT."

She paused for thought before continuing.

"Actually, I'm already talking to Olivia on another topic," she decided to reveal. "So I can casually test out whatever we decide to suggest."

Any lengthy meeting needs a healthy interval, so for the next fifteen minutes the SLT members went their own ways. Some checked their phones (through a sense of obligation, or through sheer force of habit) while others shadowed Vanessa to the nearby vending machine.

It wasn't lost on Olivia that Aisha did neither of those things, but instead rolled her chair across to where Pedro was sitting, dropped her elbows on to the table, hung her head low, and began a whispered conversation, all before the caffeine addicts had even left the room.

Later, the refuelled SLT members retook their seats for the second half of the meeting.

Pedro, the university's Chief IT Architect, was next to take the floor. As usual, he'd give a brief update on his team's activities.

Originally from Salamanca in Spain, Pedro was a near-perfect mash-up of two stereotypes. His work was predominantly analytical—concerned with bringing structure and clarity—and he took it very seriously. But he also had a pinch of romantic unpredictability, making him prone to occasional flights of fancy. His English was excellent, though the formulation of his phrases often betrayed his Spanish roots.

"For me, everything goes well with our business systems. This week we have finished the roadmaps for Finance, HR, Payroll, and Legal. Those departments like what we have done, and agree on the future plans."

This news was encouraging, but not unexpected. The others nodded helpfully, but had little to add or ask. Pedro continued.

"Sadly, it's much more difficult for us with Digital apps like *Curricul8* and *Syllabize*. I share the situation of Aisha. We need to intervene in Digital, but we are pushed to go away. When we *can* put ourselves in the discussion early, our ideas are often refused. But most of the time, actually, we don't see designs for Digital until it is too late to change them. Technology debt grows. This will prejudice us later."

Despite his taxing phraseology, everyone could quickly grasp Pedro's meaning. A few eyes turned towards Sukhi, who shrunk even further into their seat.

In fact, Pedro didn't intend an attack, he just wanted to help everyone understand the position. Through good judgment, or good luck, or some combination of the two, Vanessa had built an apolitical team, so the dialogue in SLT meetings could usually be taken at face value.

But her good fortune in that respect didn't ease Sukhi's current predicament. "I guess this is similar to Aisha's point. I don't always agree with Pedro on software design, but his main objection is fair. We don't often have the luxury to do what we think is right … as I explained earlier. What else can I tell you?" they asked rhetorically, trying not to exhibit exasperation.

Vanessa really felt for Sukhi, who'd risen swiftly through the university's software engineering ranks, having spent most of their career at Ridgemoor. Impressively, through a genuine interest in technology, Sukhi had always managed to stay fresh—keeping close to market developments without neglecting their increasingly broad management responsibilities. This brilliant balance had contributed in no small way to their promotion to engineering supremo.

"Okay," she started. "Why don't we add you to the previous action, Pedro? Could you also come up with a few ideas for fixing this without damaging digital too much? Do you understand the inner workings of the labs well enough to manage that?"

Sukhi nodded on Pedro's behalf before he could do so himself. They both knew that Pedro had started his career as a software engineer, so had an intuitive (if slightly outdated) view of that world.

A tenser-than-usual session ended well, with Vanessa pre-announcing the latest "Employee of the Quarter" award winners. On this occasion, the software engineers won more than their fair share, which went a long way in restoring Sukhi's usual cheer. Everyone smiled at Sukhi, even if Miles, the Head of PMO, looked a little distant and distracted.

Tuesday's main messages

✓ *Prioritisation is a critical and constant theme in well-functioning Agile operations.*

✓ *The healthiest digital teams work seamlessly alongside product people, with no material barriers.*

✓ *If ownership is unclear, there's a problem somewhere. Consider finding it before it finds you.*

✓ *Without conscious effort to blend non-functional needs into functional backlogs, expect some stakeholders to be unsettled.*

✓ *Non-technical product people can't be the only ones bringing backlog candidates.*

✓ *Traditional architectural governance needs a rethink for Agile.*

✓ *When there are disagreements, remember that most people are trying to do the right thing, by their own frame of reference.*

Wednesday

"That's not how it seems to me!" retorted Miles, a little angrily.

His parents must have had tremendous foresight when naming Vanessa's now Head of PMO. He was usually found racing around at a million miles-an-hour, and today was no exception. With over thirty IT projects on the books, and only a handful of project managers, there was always something going wrong—always something indefensible to defend.

So when Vanessa grabbed him on Wednesday morning and started raising new difficulties, he fell all-too-quickly into that now-normalised defensive posture.

This was the main thing he'd vowed to change after last year's appraisal, so he gave himself an unspoken reprimand, adding yet another item to his mental worry list.

Vanessa had always been confident in Miles. He had an outstanding pedigree in programme delivery, mainly from work in the healthcare and defence sectors where safety and security demand rigour. He knew his stuff. And even though his PMO experience was more limited, the general presumption was that any seasoned Programme Manager can readily conceive what it takes to run an excellent supporting office.

But now she was worried that he was overloaded. It had started to show in the quality of his work a few weeks ago, and then she caught his uneasy facial expression at the end of the SLT meeting. Today's unwarranted defensiveness seemed like a further indication.

"Miles, it's not an attack. You know we're all on your side. It's just that I don't understand how this is supposed to work. Why doesn't the PMO offer a view of Digital delivery, just like you do with our IT projects?"

"We do," Miles attempted. Then, doubting himself, he backtracked a little. "That is, all the Digital work is in the PMO report pack somewhere."

Of course Vanessa already knew this, but what she saw in the monthly PMO reports didn't seem to match what she heard from Sukhi and others. Moreover, Miles seemed uncomfortable about it all—even evasive. She had to find out why.

"Great!" she said supportively. "Let's take a look. I'm keen to understand what the report does and doesn't cover."

Miles flipped his laptop open, launched the latest report pack and skipped to the Digital section. The first slide covered *Syllabize*, the new student app for syllabus information, timetables, assignments, and exam information, intended for general release in a few months' time. Vanessa leaned in a little and studied the screen intently, trying to tease out the news from the noise.

"Miles, Olivia seems to think that we're too distant from her team these days. So I'm trying to imagine looking at this with *her* eyes, to see what it tells me. But does this report pack even *go* to her and her peers?"

"Well, no. They never asked for it. And I only distribute the reports to people who want them … or need them."

Vanessa made another mental note before responding. If Olivia and the Product Managers didn't want … or need … reports on the Digital development of their products, then who did?

"Okay. So each slide represents the status of a Digital project. It's split into five sections: people, milestones, risk, spending, and overall status. Let's take a quick look at each of those in turn."

Vanessa paused, hoping that Miles would take the lead, but he just stared blankly at the screen, so she continued.

"First, people. It says here that Olivia is the Project Manager, and Sukhi is the Delivery Manager. I guess that's a surprise to me. If this is a Digital project, doesn't it have a project manager from our Digital team?"

"Well, that's Sukhi … really," Miles ventured. "But they're not responsible for the whole project, just for the software development. They can't own the requirements, or the launch, for example. Those things have to be with the faculties."

"Okay," said Vanessa. "Point taken. But I wonder what Olivia would say about that? Incidentally, who writes these slides anyway? You?"

"I always have to finish them off. They arrive in pretty inconsistent states, and not always on time. But Sukhi's team provides most of the content."

Vanessa pondered. She wondered how Sukhi could write the status slide without full visibility of the project.

"What's next?" she asked. "Milestones. I can see a list here. So far it looks like they've all have been hit successfully. This one, for example, 'Deploy cloud web servers.' Pretty clear."

"Hmmm, yes," Miles seemed to equivocate. "Weird milestone, though. Sukhi said that the servers used the standard build this time, so they would only have taken five minutes to deploy using pre-canned cloud images."

So what's the value of the milestone? Vanessa found herself wondering.

"Interesting. Let's move to risks," she prompted. "Only one here, 'Customer requirements might change.' That's pretty generic.

And a bit light on detail too. There's also no owner, even though it's showing as high impact and high probability. Someone should certainly be owning it. But who? Sukhi? Or you, Miles? More likely Olivia … who probably hasn't even seen this!"

"I doubt she has," Miles conceded. "But look, according to Sukhi, she doesn't even recognise that there *are* requirements for the project. Sukhi and the team wrote most of them, and they can't get her interested."

"Hold on. Earlier you said Sukhi *couldn't* own the requirements, and that Olivia needed to." Vanessa was flagging now. Why did everything feel so Kafkaesque today?

"That's what I believe, yes. But Olivia doesn't seem to agree, and Sukhi doesn't act like they do either. You see why it's difficult?"

"Certainly, I see that we've got silos. And that seems to confirm something Olivia said yesterday. It's pretty confusing, but I hope this discussion will get us on the road to recovery. Let's keep going. Next up, spending. This ought to be clear enough. The graphs look straightforward, showing cumulative spending tracking to plan. Is that what you see too, Miles?"

"That's what the slide says, yes. And it's true … in a sense. The thing is, that's what always happens for the first half of the project. Then, around halfway through we need to replan and reforecast. When we do, we find that the timeline and costs have gone up by at least 50%. And we're lucky if they don't rise again later. Then, at the end of the project, the faculty tells us that what they asked us to deliver isn't really what they wanted anyway. It's mind-blowing."

"We've got some work to do here," Vanessa accepted resignedly. "Let's look at the last section, Overall status. Here we've got 'Green,' which doesn't seem to tally with the rumblings Carla is getting from the faculties. In fact, looking through the rest of the Digital slides, *everything* looks 'Green.' Is that usual?"

"Early on in each project, yes. Like I said, it's all fine until suddenly it isn't. So we see a lot of flips from 'Green' to 'Red' in later stages. Somehow, we're still surprised when it happens and haven't worked out how to stop it. We do show you these slides, but I guess we always say it's normal, and under control."

"Project-by-project, I guess it could be," Vanessa offered, embarrassed that she hadn't seen the pattern until now. "But there's clearly a systemic problem here that perhaps we're starting to uncover. I don't know the cause, or the severity, but we'd better find out. Carla wants an update next week! Thanks for taking the time, Miles—and don't be dispirited. We'll get a lot further if we face up to this. And it's not *your* problem, you know? This is something for the whole SLT to get on top of."

Walking over to the *Coffee Shack*, Vanessa was suddenly put in mind of an old sweater she'd once owned. Noticing a loose thread, she'd pulled at it in the hope of neatening the garment. The result had been quite the opposite, with more loose ends appearing *en masse*, and the sleeves starting to separate from the torso. With little to lose, she'd persevered, ultimately creating an object scarcely distinguishable from the Gordian Knot.

Was she treading that mistaken path again here?

Did picking at these Digital threads help or hinder?

Certainly, she seemed to have wrong-sided several of her direct reports … and it was only Wednesday. She didn't feel ready to meet Olivia again, and Carla would expect a meaningful update early next week.

One double espresso later, she was wandering back across campus towards her office, entirely lost in thought, when she almost bumped into Penny—Ridgemoor University's Finance Director. Both women apologised profusely, and it seemed that Penny had been similarly distracted.

"I'm so sorry, Vanessa! But good to see you. Actually, I had a question for you. Got a couple of minutes?"

"Please, go ahead."

"We keep hitting problems capitalising your team's Digital projects. We're told to expect releases on a given date, then nothing happens. Definitions are sketchy, or the deployment is delayed, and we have to reschedule the amortisation. But not just once; it's pretty much every time. We've queried it repeatedly, but it's almost as though they don't understand the problem!"

You're spot on, Vanessa thought. But she'd be inclined to drop the "almost". She was pretty sure that even her direct reports had sketchy financial nous. Matters financial were hardly Vanessa's forte either, but she could at least cope with conversing on the topic.

"Glad you let me know. Actually, I'm zooming in on a few Digital issues this week, so I'll add that to my list. I can't help wondering if they're all linked anyway," she mused. "To clarify, though, how do you arrive at the definitions of the assets we're developing? The definitions that you use in Finance?"

"We sit with the faculties who commission the Digital work to ask them what's being built, for whom, when it will be specified and deployed, and the projected lifetime," Penny explained. "Then we apply accounting rules to decide when we can start capitalising and amortising the costs."

"Got it. I think I can see where the problems might be creeping in," Vanessa replied. "Thanks for the info. Can I come back to you on this?"

"Of course. It's a nagging problem, but honestly there's no hard deadline. See you soon."

Vanessa was beginning to feel that 'Can I come back to you on this?' could become her catchphrase. It wasn't a feeling she was used to. More often, it was the kind of response that others offered to her. Nonetheless, this latest chance encounter had given her a little more background information, and would perhaps link to the other insights she'd gathered.

Maddie had a sleepover at a friend's house that evening, so for once Vanessa was commitment-free. Much as she loved her daughter and enjoyed her company, an occasional evening alone was a luxury. Some welcome 'me-time.'

She stayed at work a little later than normal, to clear the decks, before cycling home in the twilight to be welcomed on the doorstep by lovable lurcher Yogi. Originally a rescue dog, Yogi had blossomed after being adopted by Vanessa and Maddie, and now felt entirely at home. He was delighted to have company again after an afternoon alone.

After enjoying a light dinner of ceviche (not Maddie's favourite), Vannesa drew a deep bubble bath and poured a generous glass of Sauvignon Blanc to accompany it. Then, leaving the bathroom door open so that Yogi felt less abandoned, she sank contentedly into the bubbles.

Following her lead, Yogi promptly joined her in the bathroom, sinking contentedly onto the bathmat.

At first, her thoughts drifted around idly, but after a few minutes they settled on the situation at work. So far, she had far more questions than answers:

Did people outside Digital really fail to see the speed and efficiency her team now achieved? If so, why was that?

Why was communication between Digital and the faculties so limited in quality and quantity?

Were Sukhi's team as motivated as she'd previously imagined?

What did Olivia mean when she said that Sukhi's team were facing in the wrong direction?

Why did information security and architecture seem more difficult in Digital than in the rest of IT?

Why did Miles's PMO produce regular reports on Digital, with less-than-useful articulations of milestones, risks etc.—especially as no one seemed to read them?

Why did Digital delivery routinely slip, delaying deployment and amortisation? And why was she just learning about it now?

Who owns which parts of these issues?

... and in fact, who really owns Digital?

And, as Casey had asked at chess club, what would "good" look like anyway?

Glancing over at Yogi, it became evident that he wasn't going to contribute to the thinking, quick-witted though he was in the presence of a pigeon.

So what did *Vanessa* think? With twenty years of experience, she should have a pretty good idea of what was going wrong—or at least a fair hypothesis.

Of all the questions she'd posed, the question of ownership seemed the most important.

Didn't Vanessa own Digital?

If so, why was she *asking* herself if she owned it?

And why was her team taking direction from the faculties to the exclusion of all other sources?

Something didn't make sense.

Her phone beeped, interrupting her slowing stream of consciousness, and curiosity got the better of her. It was an invitation from Olivia to reconvene tomorrow afternoon, this time in the Student Services building.

A chance for Vanessa to sharpen her understanding? Or further deepen her confusion? Perhaps a bit of both.

Only tomorrow would tell.

Wednesday's main messages

✓ *Traditional PMO teams need an overhaul to add value alongside Agile product development.*

✓ *Waterfall-style reporting won't work well in Agile, so think hard about who really needs what delivery information.*

✓ *By preference, educate and encourage those with a real 'need to know' to seek information in real-time, direct from delivery teams.*

✓ *Changing requirements are not a risk, they're a given. They are accommodated naturally in any good Agile operation.*

✓ *To reduce friction, the funding model should be designed in sympathy with the delivery model.*

Thursday

The first of the 'ideas' emails was waiting for Vanessa before she arrived at work on Thursday. It was from Pedro, her Chief Architect, copying Sukhi and Aisha:

Hi Vanessa,

You ordered ideas to help architecture to function better in Digital. Here are mine:

1. All architecture designs for Digital could just go to my Design Authority before development. (Simple. This is what we do in the rest of IT.)
2. Or I could provide architecture designs for Digital from my team. (I would need more budget.)
3. We should also meet Sukhi's teams every quarter to create roadmaps to reduce technology debt. (Again, we do this with IT, but Digital does not have enough time.)

```
4.  We should meet Sukhi's teams monthly to check
    that the roadmaps are on track.

I hope these ideas also work for Sukhi.

Hugs,

Pedro.
```

She couldn't help but smile at Pedro's unusual turns of phrase and inadvertent overfamiliarity.

Through Vanessa's eyes, there was nothing obviously wrong with Pedro's prescription, but it was hardly creative. He wanted to drop his standard way of working onto Digital with too few concessions to the context. She was confident that this simplistic solution wouldn't work. It had been tried before. But she couldn't see a better way … at least not yet.

Just as she finished digesting Pedro's email, a second arrived—this time from Aisha, who *didn't* copy any of the others:

```
Vanessa,

Thanks for trying to help me properly secure
Digital. I've been pushing for a while here, but to
little avail. I can't be accountable for security
without cooperation across the organisation. I need
your help, please. The Digital teams must:

1.  monitor software and patch levels for all the
    purchased software they use,
2.  keep all those packages at the latest stable
    major version,
```

3. always apply all security fixes to those
   packages within a week of release,
4. invite our review of a full security design
   for every development project, detailing
   exposures, protections, and monitoring tools
   and processes, ahead of any live deployment.

I see no simpler way to protect Ridgemoor's
interests. But I'm really happy to help Sukhi with
all this. I know it's not an area of expertise for
everyone in their team.

Looking forward to the discussion at the next SLT.

Aisha.

Pedro's position had seemed intransigent, but Aisha had surpassed it. Much as Vanessa appreciated the warm tone of the emails, and the apparent willingness of both senders to support their colleague, neither had offered anything inventive to help Sukhi overcome their obstacles. Each had stayed in their comfort zone while Sukhi was stuck deep outside theirs.

So, what ideas *would* have helped? Vanessa asked herself.

In a typical IT project, it was in her gift to give Pedro and Aisha what they needed. In fact, their interventions were automatically invited at planned points in the project processes.

But in Digital, Vanessa and the SLT were no longer in the driving seat, and those interventions were often overlooked. Sukhi was working to order, to deliver what Olivia and her peers wanted, and nothing else. Pleas to consider good architecture and strong IT security fell on deaf ears.

Surely though, the faculties didn't want *bad* architecture?

And certainly they wouldn't like the sound of *weak* IT security.

So what was going on? Vanessa was looking forward to meeting Olivia again after lunch.

Olivia usually sat amongst her peers in an open-plan area, with ready access to the nearby meeting room where the two had decided to meet. But when Vanessa arrived, the place was deserted, so she helped herself to the room while she waited and began peering at the many plans plastering its walls.

"Hi," came Olivia's voice from behind, a few moments later. "Have you seen those recently? They're our strategic roadmaps for the student experience."

Turning, Vanessa replied, "Hi! Actually, I've *never* seen them. Good to know that you have these. I was looking at the plan covering *Syllabize* just now, and saw a few of the features that the Digital guys seem to be working on, like *CourseBrowser* and *LibraryCheck*. Great to see them put into context like this."

"Glad you like them!" Olivia smiled, clearly pleased to have a new audience for her magnum opus, especially one outside her immediate team.

The two pored over the charts for a few more minutes before reprising their conversation of two days ago.

"So I was thinking about your parting question, Vanessa. You asked what it would look like if things were working really well with Digital. It's a great question!"

Olivia paused for effect before continuing.

"In an ideal world, the apps, websites, APIs, and data we need would just magically appear as soon as we realised that we needed them. If anything went wrong, it would fix itself in seconds ... but of course, nothing would go wrong anyway, this being an ideal world! Students would love the experience, satisfaction scores would go through the roof, we'd double our applicant numbers next year ... and I'd get a massive pay rise!" she joked.

"Honestly, that's where I started in my thinking," Olivia went on to admit. "No harm in aiming high. But what we really need now isn't that sophisticated. Just three things:

"First, engagement: I want it to be clear who I should talk to about a given product, have them speak my language, and share my interest in making it succeed. That would be a great foundation for us, and I think we'd all enjoy our work much more.

"Second, openness: I want to know what's working, and what isn't ... but only if I *need* to know. Today, it's a lottery! Some important things I don't hear about until it's too late to influence them, and other times I get an hour-long diatribe about a technical issue that

I don't understand. And when I eventually do half-understand it, I rarely see what the fuss was about. Not a great use of my time. So let's say, *timely, relevant* openness."

Vanessa was listening intently and taking notes. She nodded, and Olivia continued.

"Finally, there's expertise. This one's subtle because actually the guys are pretty tech-savvy. But when there's something they don't know, they seem reluctant to go and find out. They go quiet and revert to more familiar work that they *do* understand. Sometimes that's okay, but often it will mean we're not getting the best solutions. Why aren't they keener to learn? I'm pretty sure if we outsourced the work to a supplier they'd be delighted to learn while we paid them. Shouldn't I expect at least as much enthusiasm for learning from our own team?"

Vanessa wasn't sure if she heard a veiled threat there, but didn't want to derail the conversation. And in any case, if she were Olivia, might she not feel the same way?

"Actually, there's a fourth, too," Olivia realised. "Focus. Sukhi and company are pretty hard-working, but it's never clear if what they're doing is something that I need done. They seem to infer the need for work we didn't ask for, sometimes ahead of what we explicitly need! On Tuesday, I said they were 'pointing in the wrong direction,' and that about sums it up."

A lot to take in. Vanessa had made notes and was now skimming them, trying to decide where to begin formulating her response.

"That's hugely helpful, Olivia," she started. "All four make sense, although I don't know how we got here. I'm glad you can see the expertise. I can, too. I think Sukhi has a pretty skilled team, given their budget and the hot employment market. But I'm super-surprised to hear that the team isn't keen to learn.

"I'm also glad that you see the hard work," she continued. "I worried that enthusiasm might be waning, so it's reassuring to know that you haven't felt that—even if we seem to be going in the wrong direction sometimes! But maybe that links to your first point about engagement? If conversation about *Syllabize* is infrequent, shallow, and burdened by misunderstandings, I'm not so surprised if the direction drifts.

"And maybe all of that links to your second point," she said, rapidly consulting her scribbled notes: 'Timely, relevant openness.' I wonder if we've got something wrong with the incentives. Techies won't always seek out conversations, especially in domains where they already feel expert, and especially if they know the news won't be well received. We need to create the environment that makes them *want* to. I guess that particular buck stops with me."

"And me!" Olivia volunteered vehemently. "Sounds right. But how best to do it? And is it really as achievable as you make it sound?"

"I don't know yet," Vanessa admitted. "But look, if there's one thing I *do* know, it's that Sukhi has an incredibly strong sense of duty. They feel a real dedication to Ridgemoor, and the annual appraisal scores suggest that the feeling percolates down through the whole Digital team. That's a great starting point for improvements."

Both women nodded.

Neither spoke.

Both instinctively glanced sideways at the wall charts for inspiration.

After a minute's reflection, Vanessa turned back to face Olivia.

"Let me test something out on you. You said you didn't own the Digital platforms, and I see why. But when I asked around my team, colleagues pointed out that there are aspects of the project that Sukhi can't really own—like your requirements, the non-technical risks, or the launch of a new release to students. So if it's not you, and it's not Sukhi, who *does* own the *Syllabize* project?"

Olivia hadn't heard this question before, so was forced to think aloud.

"Well, I own the business design—the articulation of what we need to achieve for students. And you're right, my team also has the launch plans, comms, marketing, etc. I'm not sure about the risks—maybe they're owned individually by whoever can best manage them, but I certainly own *some*—for example, the risk that student satisfaction is lower than hoped for. As for the software platform though, I just don't see how I *can* own that. So, I hope Sukhi has it covered.

"By the way," Olivia continued unexpectedly, "I know you keep saying 'project,' but that always sounds a bit sinister. Projects end, but *Syllabize* won't. It will be there until it isn't, and that will be way further into the future than the lifetime of a typical project. I need Sukhi to own the platform *beyond* the completion of any specific project, in perpetuity. Can I assume that's all in-hand?"

Vanessa swallowed involuntarily. It made sense, of course, but she was very aware that Sukhi's engineers had no firm plan to work on *Syllabize* beyond the end of the immediate project. Some would likely move to other projects, with little spare time to nurse *Syllabize.* A basic "keep-the-lights-on" level of support could be available from Colin, Vanessa's Head of Infrastructure and Operations, and he could beg time from Sukhi in the case of major incidents. But a follow-on funded project would be needed for further features.

"Yes and no," was as far as she'd venture in response. "We continue to support apps, on a best efforts basis, when things go wrong. But I sense you're hoping for more than that?"

"Absolutely! We're expecting to continuously improve *Syllabize* once it's live. Today's students don't expect software to stand still, even for a term. And they'll feel neglected if their experience doesn't match that of their old high school peers who went to other universities. So, to me *Syllabize* isn't a project, it's a living *product*, and has to evolve."

"Sounds like we've got a few fundamentals to fix here," Vanessa noted.

Fond of structure and lists, she grabbed a marker pen and headed for the whiteboard. The first pen was entirely out of ink, so she tossed it aside. But she quickly found another, and this second boasted just enough ink to make a few ghostly impressions on the board.

Vanessa voiced-over her see-through scribblings.

"One, we're not seeing frequent, healthy conversations about what's needed. Two, you're seeing a reluctance from Digital to be open, or to stretch themselves into new areas of expertise. Three, we're delivering a technology project, but you're expecting a living product. Contributing to all of these, I think are the facts that Digital speaks a different language—with limited relevance to you—and that we don't know who owns what. Your summary of the whole situation is that we're pointing the wrong way. Right?"

"Exactly!" Olivia exclaimed, pleased that someone seemed to understand.

"I think I can see why *some* of this is happening," Vanessa hinted. "All I can say for certain is that we've got the ownership wrong somewhere, and that's impacting the way people are incentivised to behave, day-to-day. We'll need to make some changes, maybe not just in Digital. Olivia, would you at least agree that *Syllabize* is your 'product'?" Vanessa challenged.

"Er, yes," Olivia agreed, for the first time feeling a little trapped, though unsure why, "subject to the caveats I mentioned earlier."

"That's helpful. Let me spend some time with Sukhi next. Can I drop you a line tomorrow afternoon, when I know more?"

The shortest route back to her desk took Vanessa right past the *Coffee Shack* again. With low energy levels, and no more meetings to hurry to, Vanessa ordered a cappuccino and casually observed as it was brought into being and handed over.

She took a seat in the corner of the cafe facing the bar.

The cappuccino was still far too hot to drink, but she was proud of her new acquisition and sipped it gingerly nonetheless—scalding her lips as she gazed across at the baristas. She watched the interplay between customers and staff, time and again, minute after minute. No lack of communication there, she thought.

Then she had a sudden epiphany. In this cafe, her everyday haunt, every drink had two owners.

Well, one owner ultimately. But in the process of its preparation, two.

The first type of owner was the customer, naturally.

There's no playbook for coffee shops, but everyone understands that the consumer should consider the unmet need and then approach the bar to express it. They can use the menu if they like, or opt for something different. They can even ask for advice. That done, the customer watches as the elaborate process of preparation unfolds, passes judgment on the outcome if needed, then leaves with their needs met. In that sense, they own the drink.

But there's a second owner for each drink.

During preparation, it's far more natural to suggest that the *barista* owns the drink. After all, the barista takes time to understand the need, selects the best bean, checks over the equipment, chooses the cup, tests the temperature of the milk, loads the espresso machine, and inspects the results. The barista is inches away during production, while the customer watches in anticipation from a discreet distance. When things go wrong within the barista's sphere of influence, they right the wrong. If, on reflection, something isn't clear, or a new option emerges, they revert to the customer to clarify, or to consider changes. And baristas keep the environment and tools clean and well-maintained, so that coffees of various types can continue to be made quickly and efficiently, with the ultimate aim of a better customer experience.

All this to say that there are *two* owners of each carefully-crafted drink, with two very different roles. Over the short lifetime of each cup of coffee, primacy swings from one to the other, and back again. Neither role makes much sense without the other.

And what of leadership?

Any given *Coffee Shack* barista might be a low paid, low skilled, disinterested dropout. Or they might be an engaged, expert craftsperson, genuinely interested in the problem and the art of creating the best solution—and looking for opportunities to innovate with new beans, grinders, or pressure methods. A world of difference between those two possibilities, depending on the aspirations, aptitude, and outlook of the *Shack* manager. And not something that the customer can directly change.

Vanessa felt the power of analogy buffet her sharply. How different was all this to the situation of her *Digital* 'baristas'?

The Digital 'cups of coffee' were created for Olivia on behalf of her users. She must own the need, and the mode of consumption. She could best contribute by communicating clearly in a shared language, being receptive to advice, flagging up potential problems quickly, and offering rich, constructive feedback.

For their part, Sukhi should own the considered, expert production of those Digital 'cups of coffee,' and any related setup and maintenance. They could best contribute by communicating clearly in a shared language, checking and double-checking their understanding, developing deep expertise in new and existing fields, tuning the machines obsessively, and offering relevant, timely updates.

If Vanessa was to be a successful *Shack* manager, she needed to create the conditions where all this would happen as naturally as possible. She was vaguely reminded now of themes from the inception of Ridgemoor's Agile transformation two years ago—themes that had somehow got lost along the way, or had perhaps never been properly assimilated in the first place. She was determined to revisit them right away. Suddenly, in a mood of purposeful excitement, she purposefully left her beloved corner table ... and (rather less purposefully) her cherished cappuccino, too.

Thursday's main messages

✓ *Enabling functions such as security, architecture, compliance, and sustainability may only be familiar with waterfall-style governance, needing encouragement to adapt.*

✓ *Ideally, product people should share physical and virtual workspaces with their digital developers.*

✓ *Product people and developers should expect to advance their understanding of each other all the time, the better to communicate.*

✓ *If technologists are reluctant to learn or experiment, there's a problem.*

✓ *Any digital project ends long before the related product does.*

✓ *Owning the product is very different from owning the workshop that makes it.*

Friday

They'd arranged to meet again in Vanessa's office, and this time Sukhi was early. Improbably, they looked even more deflated than Vanessa expected. She soon found out why.

"Sorry to be the bearer of bad news, but you ought to know. Tim just resigned. He came to see me with his letter, and wasn't open to persuasion!"

Tim was one of Sukhi's mostly highly-rated developers. He was thorough, fast, and full of ideas. He was one of only two natural successors should Ridgemoor lose Sukhi.

"Oh no!" Vanessa lamented. "I'm sorry to hear that. It's certainly going to make things tougher. Any idea why?"

"He was pretty open about that. He doesn't much like the environment anymore and feels his skills are atrophying. He said he'd tried to make changes but kept hitting brick walls … though I don't really get that bit."

"I guess he's just on one month's notice?"

Sukhi nodded.

"We should have fixed that," Vanessa continued. "So just a few weeks to fill the gap he'll leave. How I can help with that?"

"We'll probably need to resort to a contractor again to maintain capacity. Okay with you?" Sukhi checked. "Not that contractors ever work out quite as well as we hope."

"Of course, that's fine. You know the approved rates."

Then, she spotted an opportunity. "Hey, any objection if I talk to Tim? Given the focus on Digital ways of working, maybe he could feed us some useful ideas before he goes?"

Sukhi hesitated before replying, perhaps feeling exposed. "Please do. But, good luck! He wasn't too constructive earlier."

Vanessa quickly changed tack to the intended topic of conversation.

"Take a seat, Sukhi," she offered. "I've been chatting to all kinds of people about Digital since we spoke on Monday. There's a lot to update you on. And a lot *more* that I'd like to hear from you. Let's put Tim's resignation aside for a few minutes, as though it hasn't happened.

"I suppose we should start with communication," she began. "You mentioned that you don't get a lot of time with Olivia and her peers? But just how often *do* you get over there?"

"Over where?" Sukhi asked, puzzled. "They always come to us when they want something. And that works best anyway, so we've got the test environments at-hand if we need them."

"Okay. But I was in Student Services yesterday, and it was actually pretty useful. They have posters all over the walls explaining the product vision. Worth a look."

"I think we saw those a few months ago. I guess we're talking about the same thing … the charts with the blue timelines?"

"They're the ones," she confirmed. "But it looks like they're updated every few weeks, and they must be fundamental to what you're doing?"

For once, Sukhi let a little irritation show. "If they are, then I wish the Product Managers would keep us updated!"

Yes, why *wasn't* that happening? Vanessa wondered. But instead of pursuing that line, she suggested something they could agree on now, within the room.

"Or you could *ask* her for updates? This feels like a two-way problem, but fortunately one that either side could take the lead in fixing. What kinds of conversations *do* you initiate with Olivia and the others?"

"Vanessa, just how many resignations are you looking for today?" Sukhi asked, suddenly feeling defensive.

"I'm not fighting you. I understand how hard you're all working on delivery, and I have huge respect for that. We'd be lost without you! But help me to understand how your world works, and I promise to strive for a better working environment for the developers. Shake on it?"

Sukhi looked down at Vanessa's outstretched hand, then shook it, symbolically. The two smiled at each other briefly, and the air of relief around the room reset the mood.

"Look," Vanessa began again. "I realised something today. On Monday, I was struggling, because it seemed that neither you nor the Product Managers actually *owned* Digital. Of course, the organisation chart suggests otherwise, but when we probe deeper we see the gaps. Without clear ownership, there's bound to be dissonance and dysfunction. That shouldn't surprise any of us. By the way, this kind of thing feels like *my* problem—not yours. In fact, it's amazing that you've made things work as well as they do. Well done!"

Never knowing quite how to handle praise, Sukhi shuffled slightly in their seat as Vanessa continued.

"But naturally, because neither you nor Olivia feel completely comfortable thinking of yourselves as owners of *Syllabize*, neither of you assume proper responsibility. In this situation, we shouldn't be surprised if thinking is missed, communication is sketchy, and delivery is sometimes misaligned with intent. What's more, the dissonance is bound to sap energy levels in Digital … and beyond. You and your developers must be uncomfortable. Am I warm yet?"

By this point, Sukhi was nodding slowly. Vanessa's tone wasn't accusatory, and this felt like an accurate assimilation—even if the remedy remained elusive.

"With waterfall, you fixed a set of requirements before designing and developing solutions. The method was for us to define, so it could easily include the kinds of safeguards, futureproofing, and other good practices that we all instinctively know should bring benefit. Then we set a timeline that would accommodate them, and shortcuts were only by exception. I know we're not working in waterfall anymore. But what happens if we start to think that way in Digital?"

Sukhi paused to collect their thoughts.

Then paused some more.

"I don't know. We always *try* to. I suppose that's another kind of dissonance—this time between what we *should* do and what we end up doing. For example, we just developed the new *CourseBrowser* feature. It needs to be visually compelling to the students, and that's a challenge in itself. But Olivia wanted it quickly, so when we gave her two solution options, she went for the fastest. I get why, but it meant an architectural hack. Now there will be extra work every time a student turns up with a new device or operating system version, to make sure the HTML renders properly. We've let urgent trump important again, but no one outside Digital can see it yet. I tried to explain to Olivia, but she didn't engage. She didn't even seem interested."

"Hmmm. Well, *I'm* interested!" Vanessa replied. "But let me check—how did you explain the issue to her?"

"We wrote a whitepaper."

Vanessa raised half an eyebrow.

Sukhi understood her meaning. "A short one! It covered the pros and cons of both options. It was only three pages, and I proofread it *en route*. I don't know if she even read it. She just asked us to go for option B."

"That's a really great example, Sukhi. Thanks. What strikes me is that a technologist-authored whitepaper might not be something Olivia knows *how* to read. I'm sure you offered to talk her through it, but that might mean using time she doesn't have."

"So, what's a better approach? I confess, I'm at a loss."

"There might be several ways to get a better outcome. But it depends on how Olivia likes to communicate. I don't claim to understand her that well … not yet. But we should find out."

"Here's another thought, though," Vanessa continued. "Maybe this is a decision within your sphere of ownership, rather than Olivia's. Maybe it's a conversation that can stay inside Digital.

Great to share information, but when you're deep in tech territory like this, and the soundest solution is clear, within the principles Olivia has set, maybe no debate is needed?"

Sukhi stared at Vanessa, trying to absorb her idea. This wasn't the way they'd been working, at least not since the last waterfall project, two years ago.

"Okay. Maybe. But option A would have taken a little longer in the short term. And it would have pushed us over our initial estimate. I don't have the authority to do that, do I?"

"Nobody knows!" Vanessa replied, her eyes twinkling now in amusement. "We've yet to define the responsibilities well enough. But I think we *need* you to have that authority. You're the best person to hold it. I'm also thinking about the conversation with Aisha and Pedro. Maybe if we can adjust the balance of responsibility, we can get outcomes that work better for everyone."

Sukhi nodded. "Maybe," they conceded.

This was as much as Vanessa had hoped for in the discussion, and she still hadn't settled in her mind whether her proposal would be well received by Olivia, so she switched topic.

"Let's touch on technology expertise, while we're talking. Something else that Olivia mentioned was an apparent reluctance to tackle unfamiliar technologies. That seemed really weird to me. I'd expect your guys to relish the opportunity!"

"There are always some things people don't want to get close to," Sukhi admitted. "But mostly only obsolete or deprecated technologies. Developers don't like to dilute their CVs."

Sukhi caught Vanessa shaking her head, so decided to change tack.

"But if you're talking about *newer* technologies," they continued, "then I think I know what she means—and it's similar to the problem we just talked about. We can't afford to lose the time it takes to stumble, experimenting with a technology we don't understand. It would mean failed sprints, and no one would thank us for that. So if Olivia sees reluctance, then it's her doing! No one enjoys this inflexibility, and it certainly holds us all back."

Vanessa was dumbstruck. Perhaps she'd had a rose-tinted view of Digital because the person she knew best was Sukhi, who had always had a passion for new technology. Now she barely recognised her interlocutor. "This doesn't sound like you," she blurted out, unthinkingly.

"I don't *feel* like me!" Sukhi agreed.

Vanessa liked to play people to their strengths, but had clearly fallen short here.

"I understand," she said, sympathetically. "I don't want that to continue. Let's fix it."

She excused herself for two minutes to regroup. Checking her email before heading back in, she spotted Carla's invitation for a follow up discussion on Monday. Great, she thought. The sooner we reconvene now, the better. The picture is starting to become clear.

Striding back into her office, she realised what she and Sukhi should focus on next.

"Thanks for sharing all this," she began. "I'm convinced there's a better way to do Digital, and it starts with this theme of ownership."

She wandered over to the whiteboard, grabbing a marker *en route*, and started writing.

Or at least, she started *trying* to write. Like 84% of all whiteboard markers, it was out of ink. As it transpired, so were most of the others in the room. Unphased, Vanessa swept them all a nearby bin and without missing a beat extracted her own from her jacket pocket.

"Here's Olivia," she explained, drawing an unflattering stick figure on the board.

"And here's you," she added. "Let's dive into who owns what, or rather—who *should* own what."

"I'm up for that," Sukhi offered. "How about starting with the business case. Surely that's Olivia's?"

"Yes," Vanessa agreed, annotating the whiteboard. "Good start. You and the team can help her of course—and proactively—but it's hers to own."

"And the same for the backlog of work?" Sukhi queried, less certain this time.

"I think so too," came the CDIO's reply. "But it's not so clear cut this time, is it? We've already talked about work that Olivia doesn't recognise, but should still happen. That work might need to make its way onto the backlog. So I'll put a question mark there, and let's come back to it. What else?"

"I feel like I'm going up a level here, but how about the 'product' itself, holistically," Sukhi offered. "You know, the marketing, the terms and conditions, the money, the launch, …"

"Yes …," Vanessa hesitated. "That sounds right. But it rather begs the question of what's left for *you* to own," she prompted. "What else is there?"

"Well, the developers are with me. And I don't expect Olivia to identify with the tools we use for development, integration, testing, or code promotion. So, I suppose that's all with me, too."

Why did Sukhi not seem sure even of this? Vanessa felt that their confidence had never been lower.

"Absolutely!" she declared, keen to land at least this crucial point. "They're with you. Olivia couldn't own them, and in any case, they're used in support of other products, too. These are great *examples* of what you own, but I think we can broaden things a little. Seems to me you own the entire *means of production*—the factory that is Digital."

It wasn't a question, but Vanessa waited for Sukhi's assent before adding 'means of production / factory' to the whiteboard.

"So Olivia owns the product, and I own the means of production," Sukhi summarised. "At least in as far as the product is technological. This is helpful. Can I go away and work on this, Vanessa? I'd like to build on it, and come back with more precise demarcations."

"Yes, please!" Vanessa was delighted to see Sukhi's active re-engagement. "I'd love to see what you come up with. How about thinking through a typical week, or the development of a single feature, to arrive at a list of areas of ownership?"

"I will. I'll try to remember what happened with last month's *LibraryCheck* feature. That should give me plenty to work with. I'll send you something as soon as I have it," Sukhi announced, striding purposefully out of her office.

The moment Sukhi was out of sight, Vanessa realised that she hadn't broached the subject of the project reports that had become the bane of Miles's life, and that were perhaps no more welcome in Sukhi's team. Still, bombarding her staff with problems probably wasn't the way to make progress. It could wait until next week.

With time to spare, she decided to try Tim, to better understand the reasons behind his unwelcome resignation. With no software release planned this week, it was likely to be a convenient time, and indeed Tim responded quickly and enthusiastically. They agreed to meet at the student refectory so they could lunch while they talked.

"I'm glad you were available," Vanessa opened as she and Tim collected their food and headed to a private booth. "I was very sorry to hear that you'd resigned. And Sukhi fears that your decision is final?"

"Yep," Tim replied immediately. "Vanessa, you know I love the team, but things have been going downhill for a while now. That's my view anyway, although I know I'm not alone in thinking it."

Vanessa nodded, allowing him to expand, while simultaneously allowing herself a first taste of her overly-elaborate, overpriced roasted red pepper focaccia open sandwich.

"I found another job. I wasn't looking … I was headhunted. It doesn't matter where, but it looks really promising. They're very happy to pay more, they use more advanced technology, and most importantly—their ways of working are much more mature."

Tim wasn't one to mince words. He'd come straight to the point … in fact to *all* of the points. Three explicit reasons for leaving, all warranting some exploration.

"Okay. I can hear your enthusiasm," Vanessa empathised. "You mentioned money first, but you already know we're open to ad hoc salary reviews, so I guess that wasn't the main problem?"

Tim nodded.

Again, Vanessa remained silent, but smiled encouragingly. She was keen for Tim to continue in his own words.

"Working with newer tech is a real draw," Tim explained. "The last thing any of us want is to go stale. We want to be as employable as possible for years to come, and that means staying pretty cutting-edge. In any case, it's fun! We should be far more innovative here at Ridgemoor, but have become totally risk averse instead. Anything that might threaten delivery is pushed away, even when it looks particularly promising!"

Vanessa had already heard this complaint from Olivia, and a partial explanation from Sukhi. Now, it was clear that the phenomenon had contributed to the resignation of one of the university's best Digital developers.

"For what it's worth, I know Sukhi doesn't feel entirely comfortable with the situation either," she offered. "It's something we need to change. But please don't mention this to any of the others, at least until we can work out how to do that."

Tim agreed, and she was confident in taking him into her trust. Besides, that discomfort would already be obvious to anyone else working closely with Sukhi. They wore their heart on their sleeve, hiding little.

"But that's not the main problem for me," Tim confided. "The biggest thing is the way we've fallen into working. I mean, we're just order takers for people who don't even understand what they're asking for. The Product Managers keep vague, ambiguous backlogs, and instead of pursuing clarity, we just second guess what they want and then commit it to the code. Sometimes it works, sometimes it doesn't. Then, under pressure to meet deadlines—artificial ones, I think—we cut corners. We lose focus on quality and don't document anything properly. In our rush to please the faculties, we've all forgotten that we're IT professionals, and lost track of what good looks like."

Vanessa was momentarily reminded of her brief conversation with Californian Casey on Monday evening, at the end of which he implored her to consider what things would look like once they were working as originally envisaged. Now Tim was on a similar theme.

"We should be *collaborating* with the Product Managers every step of the way, with an equal voice. As things stand, we just let them dominate. But because they don't understand the technology or the data, they're not *equipped* to dominate. They make bad choices. I don't know why we accept this setup. I think we got Agile wrong. It happens a lot in industry, but somehow I didn't expect it to happen here."

Ownership again, Vanessa thought.

And communication.

But something more, too.

Two years ago, as the Agile transformation began, she wouldn't have heard these complaints. She was pretty sure of that. Something had happened subsequently to weaken the regime. She had a sinking feeling that she had missed a trick in gradually allowing Olivia and the Product Managers to become the first among equals in Digital, instead of maintaining a spirit of partnership. That wasn't Sukhi's fault. It was hers.

"There's something else," Tim continued, clearly keen to offload. "But please keep this one confidential, okay?"

Vanessa nodded in agreement again, wondering how many more problems could possibly surface in one week. Tim looked around the room before continuing hesitantly.

"I like Sukhi a lot. At least, I *used* to when they were my mentor. But the relationship has changed. They've become more ... *managerial.*"

The emphasis that Tim placed on his final word made it clear that this was condemnation indeed. He went on to explain why.

"Far more than before, we're told what to do and when to do it— as though we don't know our own jobs. It's uncomfortable, and a lot of the guys have become "yes men" in response. They've switched-off their brains and started making mistakes. They're craftspeople stuck on a factory production line, and I don't see anyone smiling. We try to raise these problems at the retrospectives every two weeks, but we can't find the words, and people have lost interest in trying to make improvements when the overarching environment feels so combative. I tried talking to Sukhi, but they looked distracted—almost as though they couldn't hear … or didn't want to. Sorry Vanessa, but that's how it is. Maybe my view is stronger than average, but I think every other developer would recognise what I'm saying."

This last observation was the most troubling to Vanessa. It pointed to a cultural problem, which might be difficult to undo.

"Okay," came Vanessa's resigned reply. "Thanks for sharing. I know it's not the easiest thing to do. I can see we're not going to persuade you to stay. But maybe what you've told me will help us get back on track. Do keep in touch in the meantime, yes?"

"Definitely. I've got some good friends here. Hope it works out for them," Tim replied graciously before heading back to his desk.

Friday's main messages

✓ *When stress has crept in, reduce anxiety with assurance and support before pursuing contentious change.*

✓ *Poor communication is a two-sided problem.*

✓ *Agile offers no excuses for slipping standards or neglecting non-functional needs.*

✓ *Be watchful for self-imposed constraints.*

✓ *Most developers enjoy rank and remuneration, but many would prioritise harmony, respect, autonomy, and opportunities to learn.*

Weekend

Vanessa was certainly ready for her weekend. She signed out as early as possible that afternoon, and headed home to Maddie and Yogi.

She had a relaxing Friday night, greatly aided by a Chinese takeaway and the Disney channel. Maddie had recently become a teenager and was starting to focus on friends ahead of family, but the two still shared many common interests, so spent a full two hours joining Lin Manuel-Miranda and company, singing the libretto of *Hamilton* at the tops of their voices.

Waking early on Saturday morning, Vanessa thought it best to check her emails. She rarely did so at the weekend, but the Ridgemoor students didn't stop studying on Saturday and Sunday—at least not completely—and even with Colin's capable management of IT operations, she couldn't quite distance herself from feeling responsible for everything all the time. There were no messages to trouble her, but one looked intriguing:

```
Saturday, 01:53
From: Sukhi
To: Vanessa
Subject: Who owns what?
```

Wow. Sukhi certainly hadn't spent the evening singing *Hamilton*. They were more engaged in this question than Vanessa realised. She couldn't resist a quick peek.

Inside the email they proposed two lists of areas of ownership. One for Digital and another for the Product Managers, as follows:

```
Digital delivery owns the 'means of production' for
Digital, namely:

1.  Documentation of requirements
2.  Technology selection decisions
3.  User interface design
4.  Technology and data design and engineering
5.  Integration of code, configuration, and data
    items
6.  Construction of releases
7.  System testing, automated and manual
8.  Deployment to environments
9.  Setup and ongoing management of the IT
    environment used for the above
10. Internal processes and tools used by
    technologists in support of all the above
11. Continuous improvement of all the above
12. Resourcing and management of Digital
    developers
```

13. Task management of Digital developers

The Product Managers own everything else, including:

1. Product vision
2. User experience design
3. Product backlog of work
4. Backlog prioritisation
5. Any supporting marketing work
6. Any supporting intranet content
7. Terms, conditions, and other legal matters
8. Policies for usage and support
9. Pricing, where applicable
10. Launch and withdrawal plans
11. Realisation of benefits
12. Funding

At the end of the email, Sukhi revealed their outstanding concerns:

1. I'm not sure yet what we do with requirements. We currently create them, because no one else does, and we often want to specify what's needed for security, privacy, operability, etc. — things Olivia and the others don't worry about. Can we discuss?
2. Project reporting is a worry too. Currently, I send stuff to Miles every week. It's a lot of admin, the template doesn't work well for us, and I'm not sure who reads it. Maybe Olivia and the others should be writing these things? But then, how do I show *you* what's going on?
3. Then there's budgetary planning. I think that Olivia owns the product, but then I come to you separately with a Project Charter every

```
quarter and ask to continue spending. It's
clunky, and I'm not sure it serves much
purpose. Cutting Olivia out of it seems weird,
but cutting you out wouldn't feel right,
either.
```

Vanessa liked these lists a lot. Even the list of concerns. She couldn't think of much to add but spotted a few snags to smooth out. For example, she couldn't see how Sukhi could select technologies without help from the Product Managers. Often, there would be critical non-technology consequences to consider.

All-in-all though, this email seemed a great springboard for a constructive conversation with Olivia. More to tell Carla on Monday.

She put her laptop back in its bag and spent the rest of the weekend catching up with real life. Unusually for a lurcher, Yogi demanded a long walk that afternoon, while on Sunday, Maddie visited friends, leaving Vanessa free to spend much of the day reading novels and magazines in the sun. A great way to rest and recuperate, ready for the coming week.

Fun fact for the weekend

✓ *Hip-hop musical Hamilton, based during the US Revolution, boasts a total of 47 songs.*

(Maddie knows every word of the libretto, but Vanessa is still playing catch-up.)

Week Two

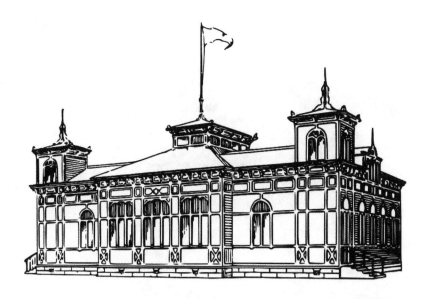

Monday

"Well, of course!" Carla scolded, within five minutes of the start of Monday's follow-up meeting.

This wasn't the reaction Vanessa had expected, given the progress she felt that she'd made in just one week.

"At the end of the day, we're a business," Carla snapped. "And IT is a function of the business. The units of the business—faculties in our case—provide services to our customers ... erm, students. And you support them in that, just like HR or Finance does."

"So, *naturally*, you can see two owners," she continued. "But take care to remember the relationship between them. Everything you do is ultimately in support of educating students ... and earning fees."

Vanessa felt unreasonably reproached, but kept her cool.

"I get why this isn't news to you," Vanessa conceded nervously. "And maybe it shouldn't be news to *me*. But since we started working with the Product Managers, it's always felt like they're the only owners in town. This imbalance seems to be at the root of a lot of our problems. Weirdly, by bending over backwards to do everything they want, we've ended up worsening outcomes for them."

"That makes no sense at all!" Carla scolded. "Olivia and the others don't feel you're bending over backwards. In fact, they think you're off on a tangent. I simply can't understand how two smart people can persist in holding such diametrically opposed viewpoints!"

"I think I'm starting to understand it," Vanessa interjected. "I've spoken to Olivia twice since we met and have been around my team, too. Without clarity on who owns what, our introverted engineers feel they can't really own *anything* properly, so just look at the Product Managers backlogs, expecting to find all the instructions they need. When they *don't*, they improvise—for example, by creating their own statements of requirements. But they've lost the sense that any aspect of the resulting product is theirs. They're well meaning of course, and certainly not irresponsible, but it's an unsustainable position. The Product Managers don't know how to own the elements of Digital production competently, so we'll have to swing the pendulum back and step up."

"While we're mixing metaphors, maybe you can tell me why you dropped the ball in the first place?" Carla quizzed rhetorically, more irritated now. "This is no different to normal IT! You create IT systems for the faculties, too, don't you? But you're somehow able to apply good practice there … at least I hope so!"

Vanessa was quick to confirm. "Yes, we are. I get it. I'm sorry. I think I can see a way to fix it."

But Carla's head-of-steam seemed unstoppable. "Think about Finance for a minute. Do you think Penny's financial controllers ask the faculties how they'd like their accounts to look? Or what software they'd prefer her to use to create them? Absolutely not! We have professional standards to adhere to. Digital should be no different."

Vanessa nodded again. "That's a good example. I'll use that. Thanks."

"Well, at least we seem to understand each other now," Carla sighed. "Call if you get stuck. And call in any case by next Monday at the latest! I want to stay close to this."

Heading back to her office, dispirited, Vanessa suddenly remembered that she needed to replenish her supply of marker pens. Since the pandemic, office stationery cupboards could no longer be relied upon. She foresaw many more whiteboard-assisted conversations in her immediate future, so took a slight diversion past the student union shop to stock up.

Stationery was one of her guilty pleasures. She always liked to have the right tools for the job, so she was something of an addict. And her ultra-equipping tendency extended far beyond pens and paper. She was a whirling dervish in a kitchenware shop.

Scouring the shelves for what she needed, she was suddenly aware of someone in her peripheral vision, peering at her. Colin, her Head of IT Infrastructure & Operations, was on the other side of the shelving, grinning through a gap in the display.

"Hi boss!" he piped up, as usual, seeming a little too pleased with himself. "Find any bargains?"

Vanessa smiled back sheepishly. She had some reservations about Colin, but he knew his stuff and was attentive to service quality.

"Not yet," she admitted. "You?"

"Just grabbing my copy of *Perfect PC*," he explained, suddenly reaching out for the magazine. "I like to stay up-to-date. Hey, how did you get on with Sukhi, Aisha, and Pedro? Any good ideas for getting Digital working properly?"

She wasn't keen on his tone. No one had gone as far as to assert that Digital was broken—only that it needed tuning. But given what she learned in the last week and was still learning, she hardly wanted to hold a debate across a student stationery store.

"I hope I can rely on you to be supportive here, Colin? They're all doing their best. We'll work it through."

"Maybe," he retorted ambiguously. "But it looks a mess to me. And I can't be responsible for the infrastructure they use, when they keep bypassing me to buy it! My house is in order, so I wish they'd stop avoiding it."

Considering his position now, he continued. "Anyway ... of course I'm happy to help the team."

"Great," she smiled, relieved that there seemed one less front to fight on. "See you at SLT tomorrow."

"See you, boss!" Colin grinned, with disturbing enthusiasm.

That evening, Maddie showed marked signs of reluctance to attend her chess club. She'd had a long day at school and an unexpectedly difficult history test. Naturally, her immediate priority had been to maniacally message her circle of friends to check that they'd all found it equally tricky.

In the end, she had been persuadable. On discovering that 'Tracey' had been Holly's answer to the question 'Who was Henry the Eighth's third wife?' she'd cheered up immensely—not least because Holly had been unbearably conceited about her performance as the girls left the exam room.

Vanessa was keen to grab a little more time with Casey if she could. He seemed strangely insightful about her work predicament, and she could use an independent sounding board.

As they entered the school hall, Vanessa could see that he was already stationed on the side benches, watching a nearby match unfold. She headed in his direction, aiming to sit a few feet away so as not to encroach uninvited, but he saw her in his peripheral vision and rose to welcome her with a wave.

"Vanessa! Nice to see you again. I wondered if you'd be here. I'm just watching this match. It's a really interesting game, isn't it— we're supposed to think of it as strategic—and it is—but neither player actually opens with a specific target position in mind. They just aim for a succession of *strong* positions. The whole thing is continuously adaptive."

Vanessa thought for a second, then realised she agreed. An interesting anomaly, and not something she'd considered before. His unusual insight boded well for the discussion she hoped they'd have next.

"Yes, I suppose so. I've never been a great player myself … maybe this is why! Actually, I was hoping to catch you. A lot happened last week, and I have loads of questions to run past you … if you don't mind being distracted from the chess?"

"Shoot!" Casey offered. "I'm all ears."

They both sat, and Vanessa began. "Thanks," she beamed. "So, we switched to Agile a couple of years ago, and at first all seemed to go well."

"What were the motives for changing?" Casey interrupted unexpectedly.

"Erm. You know, the usual ones. We convinced ourselves that everything would be faster and cheaper. There was a lot of support at the time."

"Sorry to interrupt," Casey apologised. "I just wanted to check, because it's not always like that. A lot of organisations are going for flexibility or staff retention, instead of speed or cost. By the way, did you have baseline measures, so you could look out for quantitative improvement?"

"If we did, I can't remember what they were, sorry!" Vanessa confessed. "There were a few models thrown around, and we hoped for improvements of around thirty percent in both areas. But the models seemed pretty loose. I didn't see much of a factual basis to them."

"Good spot," Casey smiled. "Please carry on, I'll try to stop interrupting. But no promises."

"Lately, it doesn't feel like such a great success story. The business—that is, the university faculties—are saying that Digital is misaligned, and lacking enthusiasm. They think that our guys are distracted, and not producing the necessary outputs.

Meanwhile, we still have disharmony between Digital and my other teams. My Head of Digital Delivery clearly feels like a square peg in a round role and has just received a very unwelcome resignation, which I'm worried could be the first of many."

Casey nodded. "Any idea of the causes?" he prompted.

Vanessa nodded back. "There are a few. At least I think so. But I'm focusing on what I'm thinking of as the 'ownership problem.' Being presented with a Product Manager who calls the shots on the backlog of work seems to have completely disempowered Digital. I'm wondering if most of what's going on leads back to that."

"Most of it, yes," Casey couldn't help replying, a little too quickly. "Sorry, go on. How do you think ownership *should* work?"

Vanessa suddenly felt like she was talking to a clairvoyant. Casey seemed to be one step ahead of everything she told him. She decided to persevere, mumbled something about a barista, then pulled out her phone to show the helpful email she'd received from Sukhi, with its suggested split of owner responsibilities between Products and Digital.

Casey leaned over to digest it.

"I see," he started. "This rings some bells. And actually, it's pretty close to models I've seen before. It's a great start. By the way, did you ever read Rudyard Kipling's poem on this subject?" he quizzed.

"Kipling?"

"Yes. Here goes. It's a little dated but uncannily relevant here. I'm going to try the first few lines from memory:

I keep six honest serving-men
(They taught me all I knew);
Their names are What and Why and When
And How and Where and Who."[1]

Vanessa paused for a moment to think. "Seems familiar actually, maybe from school. But this relates to the email because …?"

"Well, in the email your Digital guy is offering to cover the 'how,' and wants the Products guys to handle the 'what.' They'd decide 'what' goes in the backlog, but Digital would decide 'how' the work gets done. Of course, the 'how' can also affect the backlog, so it's a simplification. But I like simplifications."

Wide eyed now, Vanessa suddenly saw the relevance of the poem and scribbled something down in her ever-present notebook.

"Actually, we can go a little further," Casey continued. Product Managers will also want to own the 'why'. You know—the product vision, business case, and benefits? You've even got those referenced in your email there. And if they can, they'll want to set

---

[1] https://www.kiplingsociety.co.uk/poem/poems_serving.htm

the schedule too: the 'when'. Meanwhile, Digital should expect to own the resources used in production: the 'who' and the 'where'."

Enjoying the literary analogy, Vanessa attached quickly to Casey's observations. They seemed to make the division so clear-cut that it could readily be summarised in the six words he'd used. She imagined that much of the missing detail would now fall naturally into place.

"Looks like you got pretty far in a week!" said Casey encouragingly. "Remind me what you need me for?"

"Thanks!" Vanessa blushed. "And your point about the poem should really help us establish rules for ownership. But we have a few other related problems. Communication, and energy, for example."

"Hopefully, just facets of the ownership problem," Casey predicted. "If you went two years unclear who owned what, might your energy levels suffer too? And might you start shying away from conversations? Especially if you were a software engineer! In fact, some forms of fear could creep in, immobilising you."

Vanessa could accept the apparent wisdom of that, and joined Casey in hoping that these weren't all perpendicular problems.

"Then there's the internal dissonance between my teams," Vanessa switched tacks. "The thing that seems weirdest there is the relationship between Digital and the PMO. On a personal level, it's fine I think, but Digital is producing project reports weekly, and the PMO is polishing and distributing them into the ether. Both are uneasy about the whole thing."

"Hmmm. I guess I should check what PMO stands for?" Casey asked.

Given the level of understanding he'd previously demonstrated, how could he be so naïve now?

"It's our Project Management Office," she began. Then reflecting, she added, "… or maybe *Portfolio* Management Office? Come to think of it, we use both, pretty much interchangeably."

"I'll bet," Casey replied knowingly. "But what has either one of those got to do with Digital?" he probed.

Vanessa looked startled. "I don't know what you mean!" She felt derailed by some of his questions, but was intrigued to understand his intent in asking.

"Well, let's assume for a minute that the 'P' stands for *portfolio*. So the office keeps track of your portfolio—the collection of resource investments planned to bring returns?"

Seeing a clear nod from Vanessa now, he continued at pace. "And whose portfolio are the Digital products in?" he provoked.

Now Vanessa could see the inconsistency. "Ah, yes. Not mine, I guess. The portfolios of the Product Managers, I suppose."

"Sounds like it," Casey confirmed amiably. "So you manage them too, because … ?"

"When you put it like that, I don't know anymore! Maybe because we've got a lot of our staff in there doing change work, or because I'll somehow be accountable anyway, and we need to watch the work. I mean, we've always managed all of the IT projects, even those sponsored by the faculties."

"I'm guessing that's a little different. Sounds like you're managing delivery there. And even if the end outcome isn't technologically-based, there's a well-defined subproject which you're delivering to the business, end-to-end?"

He was right. What was Casey's background, she wondered—not for the first time. But he hadn't finished yet.

"This actually brings me on to a second point that's a little more fundamental," he went on, leaving Vanessa still struggling in the wake of the previous one.

"You'll like this one," he smiled. A presumption that Vanessa didn't share.

"Going back to the PMO, now let's assume it's a *project* office. It keeps track of discrete start-stop change initiatives called 'projects' undertaken by IT."

"I know what you're going to say," Vanessa offered. "They're not really with IT, right."

"True," Casey grinned. "We just touched on that. But there's something else. If you're dealing with Digital products, the last thing you need is *projects* complicating matters."

This was about as much as Vanessa could take in an evening. Her eyes glazed over, and her gaze glided across to Maddie's concentrated expression on the far side of the room.

After a few moments, she returned her attention. "Okay. I'm listening. So how are my Digital projects *not* projects? A project is a vehicle for delivery, and we're delivering."

"Yes, but a project isn't the only possible vehicle for delivery. For example, when your IT support teams make changes in the live environment, do they always use projects?"

"Not always," she conceded. "But those are usually much smaller changes, and often unplanned."

"Understood," Casey replied. "Just an example of an alternative delivery vehicle you already use—operational change management. But I don't want to go off at a tangent. Instead, let me ask about a few defining features of projects to see how well they apply to Digital. First, a project has a fixed scope. Does Digital have that?"

"Er … yes, in any given period. For each quarter, we lay out pretty clearly what we're going to deliver. But then every few weeks, the Product Managers ask us to change it."

"Okay. Got it," Casey affirmed. "So everyone *acts* like the scope is fixed, but, in fact, it changes all the time. Next, do your Digital endeavours have start and end dates?"

"Yes! I mean, Digital products like *Syllabize* always benefit from further investment, and actually one of the Product Managers raised this question of continuity with me last week. But we define each calendar quarter as a project, so it ends on the 30th or 31st of the third month, unless deliverables slip."

"And the next project starts the next day, right? Continuing where the previous one left off?"

"Ideally, yes, but sometimes we have a blip, waiting for capital expenditure approval or scope sign-off."

"Okay. So the product teams want the work to continue uninterrupted, broadly speaking. But switching from project N to project N+1 sometimes creates a delay."

"Yes. Just as our more traditional IT projects are sometimes delayed that way," Vanessa explained, a little defensively now.

"How about a work breakdown structure? And a specific, resourced task plan?"

"Yes, we have those … at least I think so. But I guess they don't get talked about much now," Vanessa conceded. "They were just changing too often—mainly because of volatile scope, but also because the engineers would realise the need for new tasks as they went along."

"Not surprising," Casey accepted. "And not a problem. Last question now, do your projects have a project manager?"

"Yes, they do! Well, kind of. Or maybe ... no they don't," Vanessa hedged, squinting in her struggle to find the best answer. "They *should* have. I mean, Sukhi, our Head of Digital Development is the nearest thing to a project manager. Though that's not really their role. But there's usually a *Product* Manager."

"Who maintains the work breakdown, allocates tasks, tracks activity, and manages risk?" Casey probed.

Vanessa shook her head in silence. No, that wasn't the role assumed by Olivia or any of her peers. They weren't immersed in managing the development work and would never expect to take-on that role. She felt she was losing her grip on Digital more each minute as the conversation unfolded.

"It's fine," Casey said comfortingly. "This is all pretty common, and all fixable. Your guys have preserved elements of project management in Digital, despite the shift to Agile. It happens a lot. It's kind of like a comfort blanket. But did you know that the most common Agile approach worldwide doesn't depend on using projects at all?"[2]

Vanessa didn't, and looked at him a little blankly. There were echoes here of the conversation with Tim. Was this what he'd been hinting at?

"Let me explain. It's simple really, so long as I explain it right. Digital delivers product change. For most Digital products, the level of change might wax and wane, but it never stops. Just like your live operations never stop. So you have to start thinking of Digital development as operational, not as a series of stop/start projects. Hence the term 'DevOps', by the way."

Vanessa listened intently. That much at least made sense, and it might account for some of the dysfunction back at base.

"Every time we apply project-thinking to Digital," Casey expanded, "we complicate it. In effect, we ask the developers to apply the constructs of a temporary project *as well as* the constructs of an eternal product, when actually the two are incompatible! There's dissonance."

Bingo! Thought Vanessa. There certainly is.

"What's your day rate?" she asked Casey instinctively, half in jest.

---

[2] Refer to https://digital.ai/resource-center/analyst-reports/state-of-agile-report/ and https://scrumguides.org/index.html.

"Oh, I retired a while back," Casey chuckled. "But I like these kinds of conversations … even more than watching chess."

Suddenly reminded of where they were, Vanessa looked around the room. She saw that Maddie's match had just finished, and her daughter was upright, packing up her stuff, ready to leave.

"This is really helpful. Time for one more quick question?" she asked hopefully.

Casey was upright too now, but nodded obligingly.

Vanessa rose to rejoin him. "I'm just wondering about security and systems architecture," she started, none too clearly.

"Right. That's probably a longer conversation than we can do now," Casey apologised. "But hey, why not take a look at your 'definition of done' for some clues?"

Now floating towards the exit, he added, "Oh, and think about your tax rate, too. See you next week!"

Monday's main messages

✓ *Digital does a disservice to its product leaders by taking every backlog item as read.*

✓ *The comparison of Digital to the Finance function is a useful one— would anyone expect a business unit to determine its own accounting standards?*

✓ *Confirmation bias and other social phenomena mean that highly regimented, procedurised teams often resent the freedoms that Agile teams appear to have.*

✓ *Increasingly, across all industries, the accelerating pace of change makes adaptive strategies more valuable, and precise modelling of future states less so.*

✓ *Flexibility isn't the only reason to adopt Agile, nor even always the main reason.*

✓ *A business case alone is unlikely to secure the sustained support needed to complete a transformation—belief is also critical.*

✓ *The constructs of a waterfall 'project' are largely incompatible with those of an Agile 'product', so using both tends to brings complexity and confusion.*

Tuesday

Vanessa was usually a sound sleeper. Her cycling gave her plenty enough exercise, she was sure to eat well, and as a single parent took care not to let difficulties at work cast a shadow at home.

But tonight was different.

When Vanessa heard bins clatter outside the house a little before four a.m., she shot bolt upright in bed, listening attentively in case of intruders. Yogi barked twice, but there was no sound of stirring from Maddie's room, so Vanessa didn't risk patrolling the house for fear of waking her daughter too.

She'd been dreaming about 'definition of done' and 'tax rate'—Casey's passing shots as he left the school hall—and those strange phrases still floated around her brain amorphously, seeking something to attach to. 'Definition of done' was a standard Agile term, of course, so she could check it with Sukhi. But 'tax rate' meant nothing to her. She wondered if Casey had really needed to leave so suddenly. Perhaps he just had a penchant for planting puzzles before drifting off into the dark?

With all hope of further sleep now gone, Vanessa picked up her bedside book and started reading. But still plagued by Casey's words, she decided to rise at five a.m. anyway. She'd get started on her emails early, so as to make the most of what promised to be another thought-provoking day.

Tuesday's SLT meetings were always unpredictable. Vanessa's team members were mostly respectful straight-shooters, but everyone's perspective was different. And the complexity of the technology services that they collectively managed meant that there was always something urgent and unexpected to discuss. High-time that the IT profession matured to match that of other functions, like finance, she always felt. But was that a reasonable expectation?

After an hour or so of discussion on unplanned matters, Vanessa moved to the planned part of the meeting, where the team would agree on ways to improve interactions between Digital, security, and architecture. She thanked Aisha and Pedro for their emails, and skilfully avoided making any mention of the missing missive from Sukhi.

"Who wants to start us off?" Vanessa offered, casting her eyes around the room.

At first, no one leapt to the fray. But finally, there was a volunteer.

"I guess I should," Sukhi opened. "I just realised I didn't send that email. Sorry, Vanessa. I hope this will do instead. I've been thinking about it again in the margins, but I get stuck every time. Let me try to explain why. I'm trying hard here, honestly!"

Pedro and Aisha smiled. Both instinctively gave their colleague the benefit of the doubt.

Sukhi continued. "The main thing I need you all to understand is that we no longer work to a plan. When we did, we had a design phase and made sure to write high- and low-level solution architectures, and a security design."

Sukhi paused, took a breath, and read the room. For now, everyone seemed content to listen.

"But now we work to a backlog. There's usually only a few weeks for us to absorb what the Product Manager wants next, baseline the requirements, do the design, develop and test the code, and deploy. Sometimes, only a few days. We just can't cover all the normal bases in that time. It's as much as we can do to get safe, working code deployed."

"But *is* it safe?" Aisha couldn't help herself. 'Safe' was one of her trigger words, like 'risk,' 'threat,' 'disaster' ... and 'ISO27001.' The interruption Sukhi had been anticipating had not been long coming.

"Not necessarily, no," Sukhi conceded. "Bad choice of words! You know *I* want strong security too … and good architecture for that matter. Maybe it's more accurate to say that the code is as 'safe' as we can make it, given the tight timescales."

Vanessa was frowning a little at Aisha for interrupting. It wasn't that she disagreed with the point, but she'd hoped to give Sukhi plenty of opportunity to make both the rational and emotional arguments. Suddenly, she had a question of her own, but one for Aisha rather than Sukhi.

"How safe does it need to be?"

Aisha wasn't expecting this unusual challenge, and certainly not from Vanessa, but gathered herself quickly to reply.

"It depends. New threats emerge all the time … every day. We can't necessarily pin down in advance all the work that's needed."

"That sounds like another part of the problem, doesn't it?" Vanessa suggested, cordially. "The Product Managers determine what's worked on. It's hard to explain the nature of technical exposures and treatments to them. And even if we *can,* by that point we've probably lost so much time that the threat landscape has shifted again."

Everyone nodded. A shared understanding for once. Vanessa turned to face Sukhi.

"Please do carry on," she invited. "I'm sure there's more to say."

"Thanks. On your point though, you should all know that having the Product Managers *understand* a technology exposure isn't usually enough anyway. With no certainty that it will be exploited, they still prioritise new features over fixes—often because they've already made commitments to other people. And, of course, they don't get blamed if we're hacked. That particular pleasure is shared by me and Aisha!"

Sukhi continued. "Actually, look, I wanted to keep this really simple. Only two more things to say. First, I was wondering why we didn't feel this problem from day one. Then I realised that when we initially switched to Agile, we had two things we don't have now: a pre-existing backlog of well-developed designs to match our development backlog, and freedom from technology debt. Two years later, it's a very different picture."

Sukhi paused to let this first point sink in, then continued.

"Second point, you should know that today's situation is affecting the engineers' morale. Tim just resigned, and I'm worried about a few of the others."

"It is a pain that Tim goes," Pedro sighed. "He understands very well our architecture. We have to fix this before others go. I think what you say, Sukhi, is that your work is done as soon as the code functions for the students, yes? And you don't have time to handle all the non-functional needs."

Sukhi nodded again. Meanwhile, Vanessa's ears pricked up at Pedro's mention of work being 'done' and she recalled Casey's mention of a '*definition* of done' the previous evening.

"Maybe this is the crucial point!" Vanessa interrupted, suddenly excited. "Good Digital development doesn't just mean a usable interface, or rich functionality, but also apps, websites, and APIs that are scalable and adaptable through good underpinning architecture, are supportable over the long term, have strong enough security controls, protect personal data … and probably a load of other things I can't bring to mind right now! Olivia and the others may not be thinking about those things, and may not even understand them all, but we do! And they'll be quick enough to criticise if … or rather, when … something goes wrong."

The room was with her. She continued.

"Okay. I think I've got this. Sukhi, someone mentioned 'definition of done' to me recently. Could we all take a look at ours?"

Sukhi squirmed in their seat, then admitted, "We did have one … two years ago. I guess it's still around somewhere. From memory, for a piece of development to be 'done,' it needed to have a user interface design, be coded, and be functionally tested. We also had to meet any specific criteria from the Product Team."

"The code doesn't have to be deployed?" Vanessa asked, puzzled.

"Well no, because back then we only released into the live environment every six weeks or so. With sprints two weeks long, a 'definition of done' which included deployment would have meant that pretty much *nothing* got 'done' in most of our sprints! That didn't sound great for morale."

"Okay. So it's time to update the definition," Vanessa recognised. "Let's dust it off and work on it together, to get what we really need in there. I don't want to overload it, and we shouldn't use it as a tool to redo past work, but let's at least use it to do better work in future."

Vanessa stifled a yawn, despite her evident interest in the topic. "But how about a ten-minute break first? I was up early, and could use a coffee even more than usual!"

When everyone had reassembled, now armed with caffeine, Vanessa rolled her chair across to the whiteboard and took a marker pen. She peered at it suspiciously, then tossed it into the bin without taking the lid off. She'd use her own again.

The next forty minutes went well, with an almost tangible feeling of camaraderie around the table. On a couple of occasions, Vanessa had to disappoint Pedro or Aisha by reining in their ambitions, reminding them that this wasn't their opportunity to unpick and expand past work, but on the whole, it was a hugely constructive session—resulting in the following much-improved 'definition of done':

```
- Any new architecture is documented
- Any new user interface design is documented
- Any new infrastructure is provisioned and
supported
- New code and data are integrated
- Any new security or privacy controls are
included in all the above
- All required unit tests are written and passed
- Security code review has passed with no major
issues
- Release packaging is complete
- All required functional tests have passed
- All required non-functional tests have passed
- Full regression testing has passed
- The release is deployed to all environments
```

It sounded like a lot of work, until they realised that many smaller items on the backlog would bring no architectural change, require no new security or privacy controls, and need only a handful of new test cases.

Still, Sukhi was nervous, reflecting on the long list that the exercise had exposed.

"Even if we could get this past the Product Managers," they opened, "the way we work today, most of this stuff just wouldn't fit into a two-week sprint. We'd need more automation and AI augmentation, as well as lightning-fast access to Aisha, Pedro, and others."

But Vanessa wasn't dispirited.

"Understood," she said sympathetically. "Then let's make that happen."

Suddenly Aisha and Pedro looked a little alarmed. Both had supported the change in principle, but now realised they would have to find a way to support it in practice too.

Sukhi spoke again. "Look, Vanessa, I don't think we can shift to this definition right away. We'll probably have to get there in stages, adapting progressively over a few sprints. We'll need to spend time discussing how we do it, and adapt our tools to bring more automation. Even if the Product Managers accept what we're doing, how will I make time for all that?"

"This is going to impact the schedule, undoubtedly. But I'm convinced we're in a downward spiral now, and none of us want to invite more criticism—or even resignations—by allowing that to continue! Let's take some short term pain for long term gain. I'll go and talk to Olivia again."

Feeling they were really getting somewhere now, Vanessa spotted that someone was trying to get her attention. "Yes, Aisha, something else?"

"Yes. This all sounds great, but what about ongoing security work? Twelve security hot fixes were released by vendors last week for software in our Digital stack. Does extending the 'definition of done' help us with that?"

A rhetorical question. No, it didn't. The point was well made, and momentarily, Vanessa felt they were going backwards again.

Then it suddenly dawned on her what Casey might have meant by a 'tax rate'. Despite their collective drive towards a deeper 'definition of done' so that Digital could tackle *ad hoc* work below Olivia's line of sight, Sukhi would still need a 'tax'—a proportion of development capacity held in reserve.

She explained this realisation to the team, who debated it for a few minutes, trying to iron out the wrinkles.

Collectively, they came to recognise that for every hundred days of work spent on features, enhancements, and fixes, the developers would also need to spend around ten days on 'invisible' work, which was just as critical to students over the long term, but which was too time consuming for Product Managers to understand and prioritise. A 'tax rate' of ten percent then, to allow for preventative work on the platform, and continuous improvement of the team's processes. Free of that tax, the inevitable degradation of both was already causing development delays and putting service quality at risk.

The collaborative discussion made an excellent rehearsal for the conversations that Vanessa foresaw with the Product Managers. She closed the SLT meeting on something of a high, feeling well prepared for her next meeting with Student Services, so dropped a line to Olivia suggesting that they reconvene for a longer chat this time at Olivia's earliest convenience.

Tuesday's main messages

✓ *The rate at which new threats now present themselves may intensify friction between Digital and IT Security, even though Agile methods are a great way to accommodate rapid responses.*

✓ *The 'definition of done' is the best tool at Digital's disposal for setting technology standards and protecting products.*

✓ *Investment in automation will be necessary to extend the 'definition of done' while maintaining short iterations.*

✓ *If there's been a period of technology neglect, resulting in technology debt, it's in everyone's best interests to prioritise a period of repayment.*

Wednesday

The following morning, Vanessa's welcome to work came in the form of a brief email from her boss, as follows.

```
From: Carla
To: Vanessa
Cc: Penny
Subject: CONFIDENTIAL: Digital Sourcing


Vanessa,

Can you meet Penny ASAP to discuss options for
Digital sourcing and funding.

You may need HR with you. Best not to mention to
your team yet.

Regards,

Carla.
```

It was clear that Carla wouldn't have welcomed a delay after making such a direct request, so Penny and Vanessa decided to get together promptly. No one specific from HR had been copied, but given the apparent sensitivity of the discussion, Penny suggested they also invite Harri, the HR supremo, who now went by the title of "People Director."

Vanessa dropped a note to Carla to let her know the plan, somehow also working up the enthusiasm to express interest in their next one-on-one, now scheduled for Monday.

As the three gathered later that day in Penny's office, Vanessa thought it wise to build rapport with Harri, with whom she'd never worked closely. She inquired casually about his weekend.

"Oh, it was fine … fine," Harri replied, seemingly caught off guard by the question. "Family stuff, you know."

It wasn't that Harri was socially inept, but he certainly wasn't much of a people person—despite the new job title. Vanessa thought she'd try once more and started to speak again, but Harri got in first.

"So, Penny, what can you tell us?"

"About my weekend, or this meeting?" Penny smiled, eager to help Vanessa break the ice. She should have known better.

"The meeting please. I'm not briefed."

"That's okay. Carla asked me to let you know what she and I discussed during our one-on-one yesterday," Penny explained. "Sorry you're both coming at this cold … though I have days like that too!" she tried to empathise.

Harri's impassive expression gave her nowhere else to go with the conversation, so Penny simply continued.

"I showed her the summary accounts, and highlighted a few areas we still have to manage by exception. One of them was Digital, where—as you know, Vanessa—we've been having trouble capitalising, due to slippage."

Vanessa nodded. She *did* know, even though the news was only a week old. But Penny clearly meant no harm.

"Carla's reaction was that she'd 'had it' with Digital. To use her words, if it's 'hindering Finance as well as the faculties then we need to stop, or find a radically new way of running it.' Then she mentioned some former colleagues in other industries who recently outsourced Digital offshore. She asked me why we didn't do that, and I'm afraid I couldn't give a clear answer. So here we are."

Harri nodded, more in acknowledgement of the argument than in outright agreement. "Certainly, Digital pays higher salaries than I'd expect. I don't see why developer remuneration is comparable with that of our deans and professors."

Thanks a bunch, Harri, Vanessa thought. Perhaps it wasn't so surprising that he wanted to support the Vice Chancellor's side of the debate, but it would have been nice if he'd invited other opinions first.

"Well," Vanessa began, "I don't want to sound defensive, but it's not that simple. A basic cost case can usually be made to support offshoring, if we all put the effort in and don't look too hard at the numbers. But from the perspective of quality, it's hard to think of many outsourcing programmes which are hailed as a resounding success. And that's to say nothing of the one-off costs and risks associated with effecting the change. Do you both remember *Accommod8*?" she asked, provocatively.

The Finance and People Directors both nodded vaguely. They had heard of it but weren't familiar with the details.

Vanessa saw the need to elaborate. "Three years ago, the board invited a team of cost consultants to review our books. They made sweeping recommendations in several areas. The main one in my area was that we should outsource the development and maintenance of *Accommod8*—the web application we use to manage students into and out of accommodation, and manage facilities in Ridgemoor-owned halls of residence."

Now, Penny vaguely remembered seeing the report, even though the exercise had happened more than two years before she joined Ridgemoor. "So what happened?" she asked, intrigued.

"In summary, the service was bearable for a few months, while nothing much was changing. And of course, the offshore day rates were far lower than those of our on-payroll staff. But when we needed major changes to *Accommod8* we suddenly got stuck. We realised that while the cost per *day* was lower, the cost per *outcome* was higher ... to say nothing of the delays and frustrations. We had to reverse the whole thing at a huge cost a few months later. I don't know how far your functions got into the detail, but certainly the Estates team would remember."

"Any idea of the underlying cause?" Harri asked, matter-of-factly.

"Causes," Vanessa corrected him. "Well, we somehow chose a supplier that promised the earth but seemed to have few experienced developers. Then, every time they started to work on a change, we hit communication problems. With the business problems owned squarely in the UK, and the solution being worked on in Asia, the timezone gap made regular collaboration too difficult. We were limited to one short time window each day for any rich conversation, and sometimes even that was hampered by differences in dialect and accent. We've all got used to videoconferencing since COVID, but the non-verbals still suffered, and we were routinely misunderstood. It was just nowhere near as good as talking face-to-face. Last but not least, the supplier's methods were curious ... and anything but transparent. They seemed unable to accept any change of scope without getting approval from several layers of management on their side, which didn't seem very Agile, and which created a lot of paperwork. We stuck with it for a while, but everyone on both sides started to lose faith, and burn out."

She wasn't sure why, but Vanessa was suddenly reminded of a lyric from Hamilton:

'... *local merchants deny us equipment, assistance, they only take British money, so sing a sing of sixpence* ...'[3]

It was of limited relevance to the situation, but brains don't always offer us what we need, when we need it.

Harri looked at Penny, then back at Vanessa, who had one more point to make.

"Look, I'm not saying it would definitely be as bad again, but I don't want people seeing outsourcing as a magic bullet. It's hard work, risky, and demotivates the remaining team, too. But, wait, am I wasting my breath? Is this already a done deal, Penny?"

"No, I don't think so," came the welcome reply. "At least, I hope not. Carla needed to let off steam. But it won't just slip off the table, either. I'm afraid you'll need to make the argument for maintaining the status quo."

Vanessa sighed. She sensed some support from Penny, but got no such feeling from HR's Harri, whose life would ultimately be easier with fewer staff on the payroll.

---

[3] https://hamiltonmusical.fandom.com/wiki/Stay_Alive.

"It's very frustrating," she confessed. "I know she's busy, but Carla had never raised serious concerns about Digital until last week, and now I'm working flat out to tackle them. Why wouldn't she give me more time?"

"Let me chat to her," Penny offered. "But you should, too. It seems only fair to give you a shot at restoring Carla's confidence … quickly."

Harri said nothing, but nonetheless, his position seemed clear. For now at least, he was perched perfectly on the fence.

"Thanks!" Vanessa said, much relieved. "And by the way, I haven't forgotten your question on capitalisation. Would you have any time to discuss it next week? I may need to bring one of the team along."

"Of course—the more the merrier. Just let me know when you're ready."

Vanessa paused on the way back to her office, pulling over to the side of the corridor to send an urgent email to her financial controller. She'd need some data on Digital, and quickly, to defend her intended direction.

Then seeing Miles loping along ahead, she hailed him eagerly. "Hi Miles! Got ten minutes?"

"For you? Always!" he offered, though his expression betrayed a lower level of enthusiasm.

"Great. Let's use my office."

The two settled in, and Vanessa began to explain the revelation she'd experienced when Casey discussed projects and Digital.

It took some time to land her points. Clearly, she was less well versed in the arguments than Casey had been, so presented them far less eloquently. She decided to bring them to life with an example project whose most recent PMO report they could study, so selected the ever topical *Syllabize*.

"I mean, look at the ownership section," Vanessa prompted Miles. "Last week, we couldn't quite make sense of the distinction between project and delivery management. But now I think we just need one name here—the Product Manager's. If there was value in adding other people, then we might put the name of the lead developer. Oh, but that was Tim, right?"

"No idea, sorry. Okay. Point taken. We'd have to change our forms though, just for Digital."

More evidence that Miles was overwhelmed. To Vanessa, under serious scrutiny from Carla, Harri and others, template changes seemed entirely achievable.

She caught her consternation just in time, converting it into coaxing.

"Need any help there?"

"Sorry, no. Yes, of course, I can manage that," Miles conceded, not a little embarrassed.

"Next, we have milestones," Vanessa continued. "Well, I'm not actually sure that Digital development *has* milestones—not the way we're doing it now. It feels like we're trying to overlay our old waterfall stages and stage gates on a much faster-moving vehicle. Might it be better to simply list the major items of the backlog that have just completed … or those that will come next?"

"But how would we know what stage of development each is in?" Miles squirmed. It didn't feel natural to him.

"Remember our new 'definition of done'. Those stages should now be completed as a matter of course by the developers. In any case, they happen so quickly that any report capturing them would be out of date before anyone read it. For some backlog items, stages might only last hours … or minutes!"

"Okay. That's fair. So how about the risks section? Surely we need to keep that?"

"Hmmm. Yes, I think so. But the only risk logged here is that the requirements might change. Is that even a risk?" Vanessa wondered.

"Well, they *do* change all the time, so I guess it's more of an issue."

"Yes. But wait, I'm not sure that's right either. We should be *accepting* requirement change as a fact of life. We chose to switch to Agile partly in recognition of that. Maybe the problem is that we're acting like we want them to *stop* changing."

"Right," Miles said, frantically trying to work out what he really thought. In fact, 'wrong' seemed a lot closer at the moment. "So what kinds of risks should we put in here?"

"Depends on the audience. But for now, let's assume it's a broad one. So I guess we'd want to add anything in technology that significantly threatens outcomes."

Vanessa paused. That didn't feel quite right either. Instead of just logging risks in an unpopular report, with unclear readership, why wouldn't Digital move directly to mitigate the risks, asking Olivia and the others to add work to the backlog as needed?

"Maybe some risks can just be considered business-as-usual," she surmised, "so long as we take on work to remove or reduce them?"

She was thinking aloud now. "But what about risks we can't mitigate … or chose not to? The ones we implicitly accept. Maybe they *do* belong here?"

"So maybe this is where we highlight how the underlying platform is being neglected—to support our idea of reserved capacity?" Miles offered.

"Yes! I like that. Presenting product-relevant risks which threaten the 'means of production'. Let's do that," Vanessa was pleased with such a sensible suggestion. "I guess there's also the question of whether we include the *business* risks. We could check that with Olivia later. What's next?"

"Costs," Miles suggested. "Actually, maybe we could simplify this section. We spend the same amount every week, so variations might be what's most important."

"Agreed," replied Vanessa, enthused that Miles had joined her in critically analysing the report. "But what's bothering me more is that I'm accountable for the spend, while Olivia is pulling all the strings. I'm going to discuss ownership with her next time we talk, so let's skip this part for now, and jump to the overall status."

They peered at the large letter 'G,' glowing green. Vanessa frowned.

"This doesn't seem like a fair or useful representation, when we know perfectly well that there are problems. We need to work on it. If our role is to provide the means of production and use them to deliver software solutions, then I'd appreciate a more granular view of what's working and what isn't."

"We're bending the project report template out of shape here," Miles blurted out suddenly. "Is that okay?"

"Absolutely! Honestly Miles, I'm not too sure these *are* project reports anymore. They might become something else. Let's reinvent them as we've discussed today, majoring on information that has a clear use. Look, I'm out of time. Would you be able to brief Sukhi, then work together on a modified template? I know you're busy too."

"Yes. I'm keen to fix this," Miles replied earnestly. "We should be able to start in our one-on-one meeting later. I think they'll be enthusiastic too! Thanks for intervening."

"It's what I'm here for," Vanessa blushed. "One other thing, do we need Digital reports every week? With the work moving so fast, wouldn't a monthly or quarterly digest make more sense? We can always ask the teams if we want up-to-the-minute news."

"Okay. I'll discuss that with Sukhi too," Miles replied helpfully as the two parted company. Vanessa headed back to her office, keen to collect her thoughts ahead of tomorrow's next meeting with Olivia.

Wednesday's main messages

✓ *Outsourcing is unlikely to fix a dysfunctional Agile operation: it creates new obstacles, especially in the form of culture clashes, mismatched motivations, constrained communication, and reduced control.*

✓ *Agile progress reports are often out-of-date before they're read, so if they are needed, their main purpose should be to show progress through the backlog, and the health of the production factors.*

✓ *Requirements change is a given. But the inability of the 'means of production' to keep pace might feature as a risk.*

✓ *A well-run Agile team spends steadily, so short term financial reporting tends to reveal little or nothing.*

Thursday

The week was slipping away. Thursday had come around too quickly, and the next minor release of *Syllabize* was due tomorrow.

Olivia's mood was tinged by having injured herself while training at the weekend. Perhaps, in consequence, she felt less than confident that the release would arrive on time, or offer what her users needed. She caught herself subconsciously crossing her fingers under the desk for luck.

Still, she had lunch plans with Vanessa that day. They'd agreed to meet at *¡Coman Eat!*—the tapas bar on campus. It was somewhere they both enjoyed, and neutral territory. Who knew, perhaps Vanessa was making inroads in improving her team's performance? Perhaps her injury was dampening her spirits, but

Olivia didn't feel confident even of that, given the gradual decline she'd seen in recent months.

Conveniently the two chanced to meet *en route* to the bar, so chatted a little before getting down to work.

"How's the triathlon prep going?" Vanessa asked encouragingly. Then, instinctively lowering her gaze, she realised her mistake. "Wait … are you limping?"

"Afraid so," Olivia sighed. "A small sprain. Not ideal, and it will interrupt the training. But it's not a showstopper. I should be okay in a couple of weeks. Sorry to slow you down."

"Not at all. And I like the optimism!"

After taking their seats and ordering, Vanessa updated Olivia on her progress. She carefully explained Sukhi's take on events, and Olivia began to understand why the problems she saw had persisted.

"I don't think Sukhi's team should feel disempowered. Far from it. I mean, it's their platform, right?"

"No," came Vanessa's curt reply. She was rarely so direct, but this was the crux of their discussion, and she wanted to make an impact. "In fact, this is what I've been studying over the last few days. And I've taken some expert counsel, too. Here's a draft of what I think could work …"

Watching her open Sukhi's weekend email, Olivia was a little taken aback by this new Vanessa. But she wasn't someone to shirk from a difficult discussion, so leaned towards the laptop, hoping to understand what was behind such an uncharacteristically abrupt response.

"Actually, I think you and Sukhi *both* own *Syllabize*," Vanessa explained, pointing at the screen. "But in very different ways. In my view, you own these areas, which we could summarise as the 'why,' 'what,' and 'when' of the product …"

Olivia stared avidly at the screen, trying to absorb what she saw.

Vanessa continued, "… meanwhile, Sukhi owns the 'means of production'—for *Syllabize* and all other products—which we could summarise as the 'how,' 'who,' and 'where.' In fact, you know what? I'm going to put those words at the top of the lists. They really help to get the idea across."

Olivia continued staring and nodding, finally leaning back and turning to face Vanessa, before saying, "Okay. This could help clarify things. But I'm not quite there. I have a few questions."

"Please, go ahead," Vanessa invited.

Olivia quickly marshalled her thoughts. "First, 'technology selection.' That's with Digital. But in my experience developers can be idealistic. I wouldn't want them to choose technologies that slow us down, overcomplicate the product, or add a lot of cost."

"Nor me!" Vanessa was pleased to find this first point of agreement. "So, although Digital will usually be better placed to own decisions like these, it's still your product. You should expect prior notice about pending decisions, allowing you to pitch in as needed. And Digital should explain their rationale too."

"Hmmm. They tried to do that a few weeks ago, but what I saw was unintelligible!"

"I heard," Vanessa sympathised. "Sukhi told me how they had been communicating, and I agree it needs work. You only need to know what you need to know, and the developers need to understand that communicating appropriately is a major part of their roles."

"Sounds good," Olivia conceded. "I'm okay with all that. Next question, funding. This looks like it's with me, but actually most of the spend is with *you*, inside the Digital team. So …?"

"Yes, that's right. But these lists attempt to capture how we *should* work, not how we work now. I think you should own the level of product-specific spending, in the same way that you own pricing and revenue recognition. Then you have both sides of the P&L. The product is like a mini business."

"Well, *that* certainly makes sense! My role would be much more coherent that way. But this means I should be able to adjust spending. Could I, in reality?"

Again, Olivia had landed immediately on the nub of the issue. But Vanessa had considered this ahead of time and was clear in her own mind.

"Absolutely," Vanessa replied. "It's your product, so you decide what to invest. But please be mindful that whenever we flex our teams up or down, we hit one-off transitional costs and delays. So you'll probably get much better value from a core team that remains stable."

"Yes. Makes sense," Olivia accepted. "For example, I can see that Tim's loss is going to hurt us."

"I'm afraid so, yes. We're looking for a replacement now."

"Okay. Maybe this could work, so long as I have clear line-of-sight to the costs, and understand the constraints on changing them. And I guess we don't need to rush to change the actual route that the funding takes. That could happen later."

Vanessa nodded. "Agreed. Happy to work on that with you in the coming weeks. It sounds achievable."

"Last question then," Olivia continued. "You have me maintaining and prioritising the backlog, while Sukhi documents the requirements. That's all happening today, but I still don't see them delivering what I asked for, so something gets lost in translation. How do we fix that?"

"I'm glad you picked up on that," Vanessa replied. "I've been thinking a lot about it, and this is the one place where I'd like to divert from Sukhi's suggestions."

Vanessa explained that she recognised the disjoint that Olivia had just described, and saw it as another communication failure. For her, it wasn't acceptable for Sukhi to misunderstand what the users needed and write their own requirements to plug the knowledge gap. Nor was it okay for Olivia to throw backlog entries 'over the wall' into Digital without checking that they were understood.

Product Managers and Digital would need to start working as one to get the right product outcomes—which meant much more time spent together. Sukhi would need to understand the product strategies that so elegantly decorated the walls of the Student Services meeting room, and should post them up in the Digital Labs, too. They should solicit deeper explanations of what Olivia and her peers wanted to achieve, routinely show her what they were working on, and actively seek in-the-moment steers, suggestions, and clarifications.

With that improved quality and intensity of communication, formal requirements should fade away, replaced by an enriched expression of need from Olivia and her colleagues along with the improved quality criteria in the 'definition of done.'

It was a different approach and would take time to absorb, but Vanessa was convinced it was the best way forward. The only robust alternative would be to return to waterfall development, which had failed them so completely in the past.

Olivia listened carefully, sighed, and then winced. Her ankle was throbbing again. Looking at her watch, she popped a painkiller and chased it down with a swig of sangria. These proposals were well argued, and her instinct was that they would work far better than today's siloed setup. But she hadn't expected Vanessa's 'fix' to mean her spending more time in debates with developers.

"I understand what you're suggesting, and the reasons for it. And I think I agree, in principle," she opened a little guardedly. "I'm just worried about overcommitting. I'm stacked already, so I don't know how I can free up much more time."

Olivia paused, considering her options before continuing.

"So, could we *try* it … for a month maybe? Where do you need me to sign?" she joked.

Vanessa was delighted, and hoped Sukhi would be too. "No signature needed! Thanks for listening, and for agreeing to help."

"No worries," Olivia smiled.

"There's just one other thing I need to run by you," Vanessa continued cautiously. "It relates back to costs."

Olivia frowned slightly, wondering where this was going.

Vanessa chose a confessional angle of approach, "Digital has been making mistakes in every sprint, and it's starting to hurt us and the product."

Olivia nodded, welcoming this acknowledgement and keen to hear what was coming.

"Every time we work on an item of backlog for you, we rush to deliver what you need when you need it."

"Sounds good so far! So, what's the problem?" Olivia asked, puzzled.

"Well, when we do that, as well as failing to clarify the need, we also neglect the technology. We make short term architectural decisions, skip security patches, and miss opportunities to automate our processes. After two years, all that is starting to catch up with us, and we need to get on top of it."

"So …?"

"So, we need to reserve some capacity in the team—say ten percent—to work better instead of faster. If we don't, the whole thing will eventually grind to a halt, like any unmaintained machine."

Olivia looked skeptical.

"So, you mean it's all going to *cost* more, now that I'm accountable for the spend? How convenient!"

"No! ... I mean ... yes. Actually, it is. But only because it's been costing too *little* so far. My fault. You've been getting solutions which *seem* to work well, but have a shorter shelf life than you realise. What's more, they bring serious operational risks, most of which—touch wood—haven't yet materialised."

Olivia's expression was inscrutable. Vanessa simply couldn't tell how this was landing.

"Let me give you an example," she continued. "Remember that whitepaper Sukhi sent you? What they were *trying* to say was that saving two days now would likely cost two weeks or more later."

"Then why *didn't* they say that!" Olivia leapt in, stunned that she had missed this important implication in her hurried decision.

"I understand," she nodded. "But they tried to, in their own way. This all comes back to communication—to taking enough time talking to cultivate more mutual understanding. You've offered to help here, thanks, but I also need to coach my team much more effectively, and set the context for this to work."

Olivia could be swift to anger, but was equally swift to recover her composure. "Okay, point made. It sounds like I need to give the team enough space to decide 'how' they develop, and leave more of these things to their discretion. It's a leap of faith, but if you're confident in them ...?" she left the question hanging.

"Honestly, Olivia, they're great—especially Sukhi. They won't want to waste time or money any more than you do, but they care about the quality of what they produce. There's always a risk they might misjudge just how much quality is needed, but that's where they call you for clarification, right? Back to the earlier discussion."

Olivia sighed, then smiled. Finally, she felt she understood what had been going wrong. "Thanks for being so open. This feels a little radical given where we are now, but I guess it all makes sense."

Vanessa reached for the bill as it arrived at their table, but Olivia stayed her hand.

"I'll get it this time, please. Look, I'm going to reflect on all this, but I think you can count me in. I care about quality, too."

Vanessa smiled, confident that they'd reached a critical point over lunch, with so many important foundational concepts now agreed.

Olivia continued, "What's more, this isn't just about *Syllabize*, is it? So I'll try to explain it to the other Product Managers at our next team meeting."

She paused.

"Or maybe we should call ourselves 'Product *Owners*' now?"

After her lunchtime meeting finished on a high, Vanessa decided to check her emails quickly before leaving her table.

```
From: Jack
To: Vanessa
Subject: CONFIDENTIAL - Sukhi
```

Vanessa hadn't been expecting an email from Jack, another senior developer in Sukhi's team. She read on, intrigued.

```
Vanessa,

Tim's resignation got me thinking. He and I didn't
compare notes, but I think it's pretty obvious why
he's going.

At this rate, he won't be the only one! Could we
talk?

Regards,

Jack.
```

One quick phone call later, and her fears were confirmed. Like Tim, Jack was concerned about the bad habits Digital had fallen into—an issue that Vanessa felt she was getting on top of. But again, the more acute issue was Sukhi's emerging management style.

She would have to talk to them soon, but knew that Sukhi was on leave that day. She scheduled some time for them tomorrow instead.

While Vanessa and Olivia preferred tapas for lunch, Pedro found the university's Spanish restaurant insufficiently *auténtico*, so instead frequented the adjacent sushi bar. On this occasion, he'd dodged the company of his architecture team, intent on meeting Aisha instead for an *al fresco* heart-to-heart about Digital.

But benevolent Pedro wasn't plotting a coup. He was far more interested in devising ways to help. And he always brought out the best in Aisha, who had a soft spot for him. So now both were deep in thought, determinedly considering how best to reform their roles.

"It's good that Vanessa will talk to Olivia about reserved developer capacity," Pedro had begun, little realising that the conversation he alluded to was happening right then, just a two minute walk away. "But we need to assure that the engineers use the extra time well."

"You're right," Aisha agreed. "What a disaster if she wins support, then the developers still neglect security!" she opined.

"… or better architecture," she added swiftly.

"Or compliant infrastructure!" came a nearby voice, and Colin honed into view, blocking the best of the sun. "Can I join you?"

This hadn't been Pedro's intent, but he didn't want to exclude his SLT colleague, so he welcomed him with hurriedly-constructed enthusiasm.

Now seated, Colin was curious. "Digital, right?" he asked.

"Yes. We're keen to work out how we can help," she steered, in the hope of avoiding Colin's default destructive criticism. "For example, if they only have a small reserved capacity to work with, I guess I should take more time understanding their platform and the faculty goals, and then help them prioritise the security work to fit."

"… and if it *doesn't* fit," suggested Pedro, "maybe you can help to explain to the Product Manager, who could then choose to prioritise extra work?"

"Yes, exactly!" replied Aisha. "And I guess I could offer specific security training for new developers. Maybe even one-on-one, so they have every possible chance to absorb it? Oh, and maybe I should help them to automate code assessment. It all means more work, but I'd been thinking of allocating one of the team to Digital anyway to get more focus there."

"I hope this won't distract from getting those new desktop security tools in?" Colin challenged. "They're way more important."

Aisha bit her lip. It was always hard to stay positive with Colin around. She nodded slightly, ambiguously allowing him to form his own conclusions, before turning her attention to architecture.

"And as you say, Pedro, there must be some ways that your team can help more?" Aisha suggested. "Maybe you could also train the developers?"

"I wish this. But it takes much time and experience to have a good architecture mind," he objected, stalling a little now. "It's not a thing that training can make quickly."

"I guess so. But is there some way you could train them on *their* terms?" Aisha persisted.

Pedro paused to think.

"Could be, yes! Some of our architects used to be developers, and the rest were integration, data or infrastructure specialists. Now we deliver most of those things as code, on the cloud. So I guess I could offer best-practice patterns, as code, for the developers to reuse?"

"That sounds great!" Aisha was impressed with Pedro's thinking, and it somehow spawned an idea for her too. "And how about softening and simplifying the *Architecture Review Board* so that approvals can happen quicker?"

"That could help *everyone*, not just Sukhi's team," Pedro enthused. "But the eternal problem is how people can decide what changes *need* architecture review," he murmured to himself, becoming pensive now. "We can't review every tiny change, and we shouldn't. Maybe I should try again to define 'architectural significance' so that it can become the test," he acknowledged resignedly, talking mostly to himself now.

"Why not go the whole hog? Just let them approve their own work!" Colin sneered. "I don't get why we're helping Sukhi to break all the rules!"

Pedro paused. He'd been about to argue back, given the predicament they all knew Sukhi to be in. But he thought he could see a better way.

"Fantastic idea, Colin!" Pedro glowed. "For some categories of change, we could do exactly that. Digital could *assume* approval, until they can reach us. And we could help them to continuously improve those judgments."

Colin spluttered over his soda, slightly spraying the occupants of a nearby table, who fortunately looked upwards rather than sideways, seeking a divine source for the sudden localised shower.

"No! ..." he began, before launching into an involuntary coughing fit. Leaning over, Pedro patted him on the back in a comradely fashion.

Shamelessly exploiting Colin's temporary incapacitation, Aisha leapt in. "And how about you, Colin? How could you make it easier for Digital to adopt your infrastructure, so they don't create more unmanaged 'shadow IT'?"

Still red-faced from his coughing fit, Colin was starting to get his breath back. But he was far from comfortable with the direction the conversation was taking. The best he could manage in reply was to reiterate the same mantra that the others had heard time and again.

"It's *already* easy," he chanted. "We've defined all the services in our catalogue. Everything Sukhi needs should be there, and if not, they can raise a work request so we can create it. I don't know what else you think I should do? Maybe we should just insist that Sukhi sticks to the rules instead of having me break them!"

Your *preferred* rules, Pedro thought as he stared at Colin, won't always be the *best* rules.

But his colleague had a point. Unable to wait for Colin's work requests to be approved and prioritised (neither of which could be assumed), Sukhi frequently created their own cloud services well away from Colin's tightly managed infrastructure environment. In theory, this new Digital-devised infrastructure wasn't Colin's problem, but in practice, technology was technology. Everyone would tend to look at Colin when there were infrastructure problems, as well he knew. In any case, he had the best infrastructure brains in Vanessa's team. Wouldn't it make sense for him to use them in support of Digital too?

Aisha's thought process was similar, and she was the first to respond.

"I guess the main problem is pace ... for all of us," she summarised. "Could you dedicate some of your team to Digital too, Colin, in the hope of moving as fast as Sukhi needs to?"

It was a canny question, because Aisha had already indicated her willingness to do exactly that, and Colin's team was bigger by far than hers.

On the verge of refusing absolutely, Colin suddenly wavered. He was clearly outnumbered in this conversation and wasn't sure how much more his reputation could withstand his perceived intransigence. Moreover he now began to see some personal advantage in getting closer to the inner workings of Digital.

So instead of pouting and pushing back, he hedged with a "harrumph," consulted the clock, and muttered something about a meeting. Standing up swiftly, he bid his farewells, and hurried away, leaving his share of the bill unpaid.

No problem. The meeting had been Pedro's idea, and on this occasion, he was delighted to pay for all three of them ... invited or uninvited.

Thursday's main messages

✓ *Product owners are ultimately accountable for everything about the product, but will make some bad decisions and waste time and money if they don't keep close to their technologists.*

✓ *Learning to talk each others' languages should be seen as a core skill for both product and digital staff.*

✓ *Developers rarely give their best when their leadership or management context seems illogical or irrational.*

✓ *Product owners should be accountable for as much of the contributing cost as possible, so that decisions are properly weighted, and the product operates like a mini business.*

✓ *To best enable Agile, the responsible chief officer should cultivate an enlightened willingness to adapt, right around the technology leadership team.*

Friday

"That's just not fair!"

No one spoke for a few seconds. This was a tough conversation for a Friday morning.

Sukhi was on the defensive now, and despite her healthy relationship with them, Vanessa should have expected this.

"I've spoken to a couple of people now," she explained. "I didn't go hunting for this—but it found me. I'm not saying it's your fault, but I don't think the Digital team are seeing you the way they used to. They want the old Sukhi back."

"I'm still *me*," Sukhi complained. "But yes, I direct the work differently these days. We don't have time for the level of debate we once entertained. We have hard deadlines every two weeks."

Vanessa wasn't an Agile expert, but she knew this wasn't right. And she suspected Sukhi knew it too, deep down. She had to find a way to surface that knowledge.

"So the Product Managers give you deadlines?" she asked. "They tell you when each backlog item must complete?"

"Often, yes," Sukhi agreed. "They make commitments to the faculty stakeholders. And even when they *don't*, I can still feel them tapping their watches at us."

Vanessa wondered just how much of the watch tapping was real, and how much imagined. If anything, she'd seen more evidence of Sukhi declaring their own deadlines than of the faculties imposing them.

"Okay," she coaxed gently. "But how do the Product Managers know how long each backlog item will take? I mean, sometimes they can make a good guess, but more often, their tech skills won't get them close. Or am I missing something?"

Sukhi shifted uncomfortably, unable to disagree, and visibly distressed by the question. It took them a few seconds to respond—and when they, did the words came *sotto voce*.

"Well ... we *tell* them."

Vanessa paused for effect before responding, hoping to add emphasis to Sukhi's whispered words. Then she sought clarification.

"So you estimate the work, then tell them when they can expect it to be done?"

"Yes. But look, we have to be frugal in our estimates. They clearly don't understand why technology is so difficult to master. If we're not super-efficient, they'll just outsource again."

Here it was. The source of the personnel problems. Keen always to please the faculties, the only option Sukhi had seen was to cut costs and micromanage everything—irrespective of the implications. They weren't feeling secure in their role, and the consequences were being felt right around Digital.

Admittedly, Sukhi's knowledge of Ridgemoor's apps was unequalled, but shadowing all activity wasn't a scalable way to work, and it was clearly upsetting everyone. The team had started to feel controlled and disempowered. Where everyone used to apply themselves to the smartest solution, now they just lowered their heads and looked blankly at Sukhi, awaiting the next order.

Fortunately, Vanessa knew Sukhi well enough to realise that this was not a situation they had sought. Sukhi was a keeper, so she was prepared to invest time in a turnaround.

"I'm looking very differently at Digital now," she began. "We're not in a waterfall world, with hard end dates and countless complexities compounding slippage. I spoke to Olivia yesterday, and it seemed to go really well. At a high level, she understands the problems and is prepared to support quality over quantity. That means we can estimate realistically, accommodating the reserved capacity we discussed at our SLT meeting."

Sukhi blinked twice, pleased with the news, but plagued by sudden uncertainties about its implementation.

Vanessa continued, "I'd prefer not to lose any more good developers, and the risk is palpable. I've seen you at your best, leading people respectfully, and I'd like you back there ASAP. So here's my question for you, Sukhi: Are you willing to stick around and help me finish the unfinished transformation?"

Sukhi blinked again. "Meaning?"

"We need to change the way we work … right away. Starting on Monday, we'll deliver *Syllabize* differently. Could Jack or one of the others take over Tim's duties? And can you step away from development and move closer to me? Our job will be to tune the 'means of production,' not to produce. We'll create the enabling environment in which our professional developers feel empowered and motivated to design and deliver the best solutions, in close collaboration with the Product Owners."

Sukhi's eyes were glistening now. They were clearly moved by the message. This was a rebuke but also a second chance, and a glimpse of an escape route from the private hell that had closed in on Sukhi in recent months. Any engineer who is unable to create or improve the world around them can't hope to enjoy their job, and Sukhi was no exception.

"Of course!" came the relieved reply.

After a challenging morning, Vanessa was more tired than she would care to admit. As a natural introvert, heated conversations were draining for her, and she longed for the end of the day.

She resolved to go home at four p.m., and had begun to pack up when she saw two new incoming emails. The first ran as follows:

```
From: Miles
Cc: Sukhi
To: Vanessa
Subject: Product Reporting


Vanessa,

Sukhi and I had to reschedule Wednesday's one-on-
one, so met this afternoon instead. After your
steer, we found it pretty easy to arrive at a
skeleton report for Digital products. It's not much
like the project report, because we focused on the
'means of production' rather than the product
itself. The structure is as follows:

1.  Product name & owner
2.  Development health - Morale, backlog length,
    estimate accuracy, escaped faults
3.  Technology risk - Unmanaged tech. debt and
    other threats beyond the current backlog
4.  Main backlog items done / to do next
5.  Costs - no. of teams / developers, £££ per
    sprint, reserved capacity level
```

We'd love to know your thoughts.

Thanks,

Miles & Sukhi.

P.S. We also debated what role remains for the PMO if Digital doesn't do projects. We're toying with the idea that it could become a 'Delivery Enablement Office' with a remit to support Sukhi as well as the rest of your teams — albeit in a different way.

Vanessa smiled and turned her attention to the second email. It contained a partial view of the finance data she'd requested on Wednesday. She hurriedly forwarded it to Olivia, along with a few prepared questions. Then she flipped her laptop closed, donned her cycle helmet, and headed home.

Friday's main messages

- ✓ *Some senior technologists will defer too much to 'the business,' forgetting that they are a critical part of it.*

- ✓ *Healthy Agile thrives on constructive challenge.*

- ✓ *Estimation is a critical skill in digital, and an important focus area for continuous improvement.*

- ✓ *Developers are creators at heart, welcoming sensible boundaries and support, but resenting micromanagement.*

Weekend

That evening, Maddie had friends over to watch a movie. They'd chosen a teen drama, with characters a little older than they were. Vanessa thought she could excuse herself—in fact, she assumed it would be preferred.

Time to reflect again over a longish bath. She decided to take the bottle of wine with her this time, just … er … in case the girls decided to help themselves to it. No, really.

Originally a nervous rescue dog—but now just nervous—Yogi wasn't fond of crowds so opted to go with her, settling as usual on the mat alongside the bath.

"Well?" she interrogated her pet lurcher, as she waited for the bath to fill. "What did you make of the week?"

Yogi's eyes glassed over, then he tilted his head to one side before scratching his right ear rapturously.

"Well, *that's* ambiguous!" she teased. "Do I have to work it out for myself again?"

She eased into the bubbles before meditating silently for a few minutes, but it wasn't long before the people and problems at work floated to the foreground of her mind. After twice pushing them away she resigned herself to the inevitable, and took a quick mental inventory of the week's wins:

She seemed to have convinced Olivia to take fuller ownership of Syllabize, *while simultaneously regaining sufficient ground for Sukhi to influence the 'means of production.'*

She'd just about made the case for 10% reserved capacity in Digital.

She was now armed with an invaluable shorthand for the intended division of Digital responsibilities: Why-What-When plays How-Who-Where.

Pedro, Aisha, and Penny all seemed supportive.

The SLT had coalesced around an improved 'definition of done,' which would help the team maintain quality in future development work.

Sukhi now understood and accepted that their management style had to change.

Miles and Sukhi recognised that project-style reporting was of limited use in a product context, and had proposed something more valuable which could mature over time.

… and, lo and behold, she hadn't actually been fired yet!

On the other hand:

Would Olivia be able to convince the other Product Managers to play-along with the planned changes?

Would her guesstimate of 10% reserved capacity sufficiently revitalise the Digital platforms?

Would Aisha and Pedro still struggle to keep pace with Sukhi, for as long as their roles remained unreformed?

Would Colin help, hinder, or just heckle?

How would she resolve Penny's capitalisation problem?

How could she head off another round of knee-jerk outsourcing? Was she even right to?

And how easily would Sukhi be able to replace Tim—and head off others' resignations—especially with Harri's support in question?

Suddenly, Vanessa realised that her shoulders were tense, and the bath was lukewarm at best. In response, she drew some more hot water and topped-up her wine (just in case the girls somehow got hold of it) before closing her eyes. She took a deep breath, then slowly exhaled. Her whole body relaxed, and she slid into the bubbles.

She'd focus on the positives.

She could do this.

Roll on the next Carla conversation.

Fun fact for the weekend

✓ *Lurchers are not a true dog breed. In fact, the term applies to any hybrid of a sighthound (such as a greyhound) with any herding dog or terrier.*

(As a rescue dog, Yogi is unable to elucidate us with details of his heritage. We imagine he never thought to ask his parents about this, and sadly they're no longer on the scene.)

Week Three

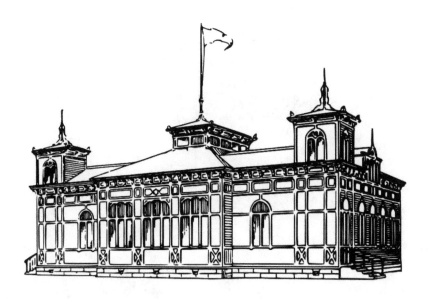

Monday

"But they don't *want* that!" Sukhi objected. "They're not *managers*."

Harri had called first thing on Monday morning, just as Sukhi was settling in at their desk. He'd explained there was a problem with Sukhi's plan to hire a replacement for Tim. The "People" team was to introduce a new remuneration policy imminently, linking pay more tightly to seniority and breadth of responsibility. Academic staff weren't covered by the changes, but everyone in the supporting functions *was*. Of course, that included Digital.

Sukhi knew it wouldn't be possible to hire suitably skilled staff at the new capped rates, so had put that argument back to Harri.

The People Director's only suggestion was a workaround wherein new staff were classed as managers or directors to allow higher remuneration. But this would also require them to assume management responsibilities, take on larger teams, and manage budgets. This wouldn't appeal to the kind of candidate Sukhi wanted to attract, and besides, it would eat into the time available for real product development.

Harri was irritated that his new policy was already being challenged.

"With respect," he protested, "it doesn't really matter if they *want* to be managers. The kind of salary you propose would *make* them managers … by definition. That's how it will work now. And it wouldn't be fair on others at that grade to excuse some people their responsibilities just because they don't fancy fulfilling them."

This seemed like a remarkably retrograde step, but Sukhi felt stuck. The timing of this new policy was unfortunate, coming just when they desperately needed to replace Tim. But evidently, they would have to back off, at least for now.

"This is crazy! Let me talk to Vanessa and come back to you." Sukhi announced in frustration, before hanging up.

Pedro had engaged with the difficulties of Digital far more than most of his peers—perhaps even as much as Vanessa had.

He was keen to help, and uncomfortably conscious of having not yet devised a way for Digital to architect well at pace.

The traditional approach to architectural governance was simply to build an ivory tower of principles, standards, authorities, and review boards, then require every project to bow unto it whenever anything changed. Now, he recognised how impractical that was for Sukhi, and wasn't content to be so inflexible.

An alternative approach offering far greater responsiveness might be to station one of his architects inside Digital. But with such a small team, that simply wasn't an option for Pedro.

No, he would need to find a way to allow the developers more architectural autonomy. And this brought him right back to 'architectural significance'—a loose concept that, on reflection, he realised he'd often hidden behind—but one for which no useful definition was readily available. If he *could* define it, any developer should be able to make a fair judgement about when deeper architecture involvement should apply.

He was determined that the problem wouldn't get the better of him, so although usually keen to protect his weekends, he'd spent some of Sunday morning discussing the problem with a respected former colleague who always seemed to be one step ahead of him. The conversation had been immensely helpful to Pedro, giving him the bones of an idea which he elaborated on alone. He was keen to share it immediately, so Sukhi was pleased to find the following email at the top of their inbox on Monday morning.

From: Pedro
To: Sukhi
Subject: Architectural Significance

Hi Sukhi,

I have been taking the opinions of others to define 'architectural significance.'

For me, it is important, because when we understand it in the same way, you will be able to see it without me there. Then, if a change is 'significant' we can review it. And if not, no delay is needed.

You will expect a long list of criteria for 'significance.' But in truth, I could never write them all down. There are too many considerations. You would tire reading them. There is an easier way to think about it …

My job is only to ensure that we have the right architecture to support the university's technology ambitions over the long term. So, a change is only 'architecturally significant' if it makes future changes more difficult than they could be, by slowing them down, adding cost, or compromising quality. In these cases, we should collaborate before development.

Logically then, anything you do which does not hinder future change is not 'architecturally significant.' There is no need to discuss these with me unless you want to.

What do you think? If you agree, I can create some worked examples to help others understand.

Hugs,

Pedro.

Driving Maddie to her chess club that evening, Vanessa found herself anticipating the tone of her forthcoming discussion with Casey—assuming he attended tonight. As usual, she had countless questions she wanted to try out on him.

They were running late because Maddie had volunteered to cook dinner, and Vanessa had underestimated the time it would take to restore the ravaged kitchen.

On arrival at the school, Maddie went in search of her first match, while Vanessa cast her eyes around the hall searching for Casey— eventually spotting him at the back of the room. She noted that, unlike most people, he seemed to choose a different place to sit on each visit.

Unfortunately, he was already deep in conversation with another parent, and she couldn't catch his eye. She hoped to chat with him later if possible, but she didn't wish to invade. Balancing those needs, she adopted a side bench some distance away, taking care to stay in clear line of sight.

Checking her emails while she waited, she was reminded of Sukhi's recruitment wranglings. Although they'd exchanged messages that day, she'd been unable to intervene usefully after a string of meetings prevented a proper discussion.

Normally, she would also have seen Carla today, and she'd been eagerly anticipating that conversation. But Carla had rescheduled.

They would now meet on Wednesday instead, and then only briefly.

Mulling these things over in her mind she jumped at Casey's sudden interruption.

"Hey there! How's it going?"

Vanessa smiled and greeted him, embarrassed at her skittishness. She'd never thought of herself as nervous, but certainly, the stakes were rising, so perhaps she was more stressed than she realised.

"I'm glad you're here. Please, take a seat."

But Casey needed no invitation, and was already half seated next to her, seemingly eager to hear her news. She began briefing him on the previous week's activities.

"Sounds like great progress again!" he enthused. "Especially in getting both the development and product teams thinking differently about their own and each others' accountabilities."

"Thanks!" Vanessa acknowledged. "I was happy with that, too." She found the slightest positive appraisal hugely encouraging, coming as it did from someone so evidently expert.

"And thanks for the prompts on 'definition of done' and 'tax rate.' They threw me for a while, but definitely got us thinking in the right direction."

"Glad it helped," Casey smiled. "Let me start with a question, if I may ... what do you really want to achieve here?"

She was puzzled. This seemed like a first-order question—inappropriate at their third encounter. Then she remembered. "Ah yes, I never really answered your 'what does good look like' question, did I? Sorry about that. Erm. I suppose it's better business outcomes from Digital?"

Casey raised a sceptical eyebrow. "I guess so. But isn't that more obviously the goal of the Product Owners and the developers who work on their backlogs?"

"I guess so," Vanessa hesitated, beginning to feel a little confused again. She'd spent so many years as a technology leader trying to refocus tech teams on the business problem, and away from technology niceties. Was Casey now undermining that noble intent?

"I'm not saying you should ignore outcomes," he smiled. "That would be pretty disastrous, wouldn't it?"

Vanessa relaxed a little. Perhaps she could handle this conversation after all.

"It's just that there's a more important focus for the technology leader," he explained. "Think about the phrase from that email you showed me? The one that headlined Digital's accountabilities? Right before I started talking about Kipling."

"The 'means of production'?" Vanessa reminded herself.

"Right," Casey confirmed. "That's your bag. The 'means of production.' And what *are* those 'means'?"

"Well, all the stuff we use to develop products, directly and indirectly. Tools, information, processes … and people of course."

"Right again! With people being the most important factor. The rest are only there because *people* put them there, and those same people could just as easily change or remove them. In fact, they will, sooner or later."

"So my main job is people?" Vanessa queried. This didn't seem too revolutionary.

"Yep," he replied. "But in the Agile context that you've swung over to—with a staff of intelligent knowledge workers—it's not just about pay, rations, and rewards. Knowingly or unknowingly, you've signed up to an organisational system that thrives on commitment, collaboration, and creativity. That same system collapses under the weight of traditional management methods."

This resonated for Vanessa. "Interesting. Maybe we're seeing some of that already. We actually had a couple of disgruntled developers recently, and one even resigned. When we asked the reasons, micromanagement was front and centre."

"Not so surprising. Look, to get this right, you have to stop telling people what to do. You don't even have to *know* what they should do—the world is way too complicated for anyone to know everything. Instead, your job is to create the *conditions* for them to thrive, applying the best of themselves. To be their 'servant leader'."

Vanessa paused. She'd heard the term before, but never in quite this context. She nodded, trying to take it all in. "So I should be managing with less management?"

"Exactly! Hey, that's really well put—I might steal it," he replied. "But it takes a while to adjust to. To help, I've used techniques like ditching organisations charts, or even drawing them upside down with the leaders *underneath* their staff, supporting and enabling them. And it all starts with making sure they feel psychologically safe."

"Psychologically safe?" Vanessa chanted back at Casey, mechanically. Again, she'd heard the term but had never yet had occasion to internalise it.

"Yep. You know—secure in the role, socially included, respected, confident speaking out, able to admit that they don't know ... or got it wrong, entitled to fail and learn. This stuff is up top in Maslow's famous 'hierarchy of needs' and should be entry stakes for knowledge workers now. They rightly expect to work in a safe environment. Without that safety, everyone is too busy watching their backs and accepting crazy orders without thinking properly about what they're actually doing, or why. There's little or no concentrated creativity, work doesn't flow. Your job is to create a safe, shared, energised studio in which creative, professional work happens naturally."

Vanessa was listening intently.

"But don't forget that ensuring clear direction and equipping staff are also part of supporting and enabling," he continued. "In fact, there's this story about a guy with a submarine, who … ah well, let's leave that for another day."

Seeing some of the players packing up now, Vanessa checked her watch. She realised that they'd timed out without her mentioning the risk of outsourcing. She quickly briefed Casey.

"It's a common response from the C-suite," he empathised, as he rose to leave. "But it sounds like you're on the right track now, so outsourcing would likely do more harm than good. I've never known an organisation to fix systemic problems through outsourcing alone."

Vanessa also stood and glanced across at Maddie, who was now looking expectant. "That's my view, too! But good to get a second opinion," she managed, just before Casey disappeared into the darkness again.

Monday's main messages

✓ *Failing to pay market rates is a false economy, because a stronger developer can be several times as productive as a weaker one.*

✓ *Traditional architecture functions should be reformed for Agile, and in particular, must devise ways to expedite good architectural decisions.*

✓ *The best Digital leaders don't determine or drive the detail, but instead act as 'servant leaders'—envisioning, enabling, and offering a psychological safety net.*

Tuesday

"That's a weird definition!" Colin objected, at Tuesday's SLT meeting, when Pedro started to explain his version of 'architectural significance'. "Surely architecture is the way that technology components are laid out and connected? It's not about change."

Much as Pedro appreciated listening to Colin tell him what architecture was, enough was enough. "Look, Colin, we're trying to solve a real problem!"

The Hamilton lobe in Vanessa's brain fired up again, singing silently to her:

"… that was a real nice declaration. Welcome to the present, we're running a real nation. Would you like to join us?"[4]

Oblivious to Vanessa's earworm, Pedro continued impassioned.

"I know what architecture is, but the important thing is to form a useful definition of 'significance' so that we can futureproof our systems. I'm sure that's something you believe?"

Colin harrumphed, seemingly offended at the idea of other people having valid arguments. "Okay," he conceded. "Go ahead."

Now indulged with Colin's kind approval to voice his views, Pedro was sure to make the most of it. He elaborated on the idea, with Sukhi's support, and gave a few examples to aid everyone's understanding.

"Just one more example," he said in conclusion. "Say Sukhi deploys a new server into one of our cloud providers' landing zones, but the other provider is where most of our current workloads are … and we're about to standardise on that. What happens?"

"I get my wrists slapped for allowing more shadow IT!" Colin leapt in, sardonically, and then wished he hadn't spoken. The room was against him today.

---

[4] https://hamiltonmusical.fandom.com/wiki/Cabinet_Battle_1.

"I guess we put at risk our bulk discounts, reduce availability, and maybe end up moving it over later on at extra cost?" Sukhi speculated, far more constructively.

"I think so," Pedro replied. "And to you, it's not important which cloud you use, most of the time, right?"

"For basic services, it doesn't matter to us," Sukhi agreed. It was a simple example, but conveyed the wider concept well.

"Actually," Pedro turned to Colin now, "this is an area where you could really revolutionise the way we enable Digital—by offering a broad, dynamic catalogue of instant access services, which are cost effective at a corporate level, as well as secure, scalable, and highly available."

Colin didn't reply, but looked more pensive than usual, and even took a few notes.

Pedro continued. "What I'm really saying is that architecture is just structure. It's important that it's right, when you need it. But it's inflexible. So the *real* goal of my team is to help you have less of it."

Vanessa was listening carefully, and grinned in amusement at this last point. She couldn't help drawing parallels with her most recent chess club conversation.

"This is fascinating, Pedro. Thanks for putting so much thought into it, and for setting Colin up to do the same. What you're saying is that, in Digital, and perhaps elsewhere, the goal of the modern architecture team is to reduce the amount of architecture?"

Pedro nodded, smiling. He was very comfortable with that conclusion. The reduction of architecture was a laudable goal. If it ultimately meant a smaller architecture team then so be it. In the meantime, the architects would be learning a very marketable soft skill—how to operate effectively alongside modern Agile development.

"What's really weird," Vanessa continued, "is that last night I came to a similar-sounding conclusion of my own—that the management of Digital also needs less management!"

Everyone turned to face her. Colin began wondering how many of them would still have jobs this time next week.

Having paused for just long enough to create dramatic suspense, Vanessa elaborated, explaining some of what she came to understand the previous evening. It was a logical corollary to the discussions that Sukhi, Pedro, Miles, and even Colin had already been having, so no one objected too much once the dust had settled on the conversation. But Sukhi had a question.

"I hope this doesn't mean we should also develop with fewer developers?" they asked, a little fearfully. "I still haven't got my hiring request past Harri."

Vanessa thought about this for a moment.

"If anything, I think the opposite is the case," she opined. "We want to maximise the number of people doing real work, per unit of cost. I'll keep trying to reach Harri … and I'll raise it with Carla too."

Their Digital leadership musings occupied much of the remainder of the meeting, and as it ended, Vanessa asked everyone for their reflections. For once, they all concluded it was a good use of their time, and she closed the SLT happy to have flushed out and fixed a few more open issues.

Meanwhile, on the other side of campus, a related debate was rumbling—this time presided over by Olivia. Although not officially the leader of the product team, she was respected, and even admired by some of her peers. So those present had welcomed the discussion that she opened partway through their regular meeting.

"So you see," she recapped. "If we're going to get the best out of Vanessa's Digital team, we've got to get these responsibilities right."

She cast her eye around the room, seeking assent before continuing.

"The way I see it now, we should decide what goes in each product, for what purpose, and where that goes in the priorities. Our aim is to *do the right things* with the product. But correspondingly, we should trust Digital to *do the things right*—working out how to balance quality and cost to meet our needs in the longer term, and how to continuously improve that."

Now, she felt a ripple of reactions around the room. But everyone was still considering what she'd said and what they thought about it. No one else was ready to speak, so Olivia carried on.

"Unfortunately, what I suspected—but didn't understand until last week—was that Digital has let all that stuff slide. Even though *we* think we're friendly and patient, they're still feeling pressure to put new features and fixes ahead of absolutely everything else."

"Which sounds okay, doesn't it?" interjected Abhi, the owner of the *Accommod8* webapp. "I mean, that's what it's all about."

"Yes and no," returned Bea, the recent recruit who spearheaded *RidgemoorAdmit*. "We had a similar problem at my last place. It's fine for a few months, but then the consequences of the neglect start to bite. We actually got to a stage where we couldn't keep the platform secure anymore because it hadn't been well-maintained, and we had to put the backlog on hold for three solid months while the Digital guys ran a gauntlet of risky upgrades. Unfortunately, by that point, some of the developers who best understood the newly-upgraded components had moved on, so we also suffered some unplanned outages while everyone stood around scratching their heads."

Charlie, *Curricul8* supremo, was the next to contribute. "We had a documentation problem in my last company. The developers felt so busy that they never took time to write anything down. They said that the code was self-explanatory anyway … right up until the point where a major change was needed, when suddenly it wasn't. Then they just went quiet, and everything took twice as long as originally estimated! In fact, I wouldn't be surprised if we had the same problem here."

Everyone turned to face Charlie. Most nodded. That certainly rang true.

Olivia spoke next, to regain the attention of the room. "Helpful examples, thanks. It seems we've unwittingly rendered Digital powerless to do what they know is right. We've taken too little time explaining our product visions and roadmaps, so Digital is finding it hard to make good judgments of their own or even to push back when they fear we're going the wrong way. Meanwhile, we've been feeling powerless too—unable to get what we need for our products."

She paused to let that sink in, then continued.

"I think we can salvage the situation by spending more time having rich conversations with the Digital teams, and by empowering Sukhi to do it *right*, instead of just doing it fast."

"But that means delays, yes?" began Abhi. "What about our deployment plans?"

Olivia took a deep breath. This was the main objection she'd been expecting.

"Yes. Vanessa suggests we'll see velocity fall by around ten percent," she opened. "But I think that's just an intelligent guess. I'm not sure anyone can be certain until we try it. Actually, I suspect the impact will be even greater because they're also planning to extend the 'definition of done' to stop further rot in future releases."

It was sobering news. Everyone in the room kept a release roadmap that might slow or slip if they accepted this new way of working. And most of those roadmaps had been shared outside the team, creating expectations in executive ranks. Some had even been published openly, so were now visible to the entire student body.

"This is the crux of the issue," Olivia offered. "But I know where *I* stand. Our releases are already slipping beyond our control, so 'do nothing' isn't really an option. We have to make a systemic change for the longer-term good of Ridgemoor. I believe that if we don't make this change, we'll see far more unplanned delays. So, what do you all think?"

The group tossed around the pros and cons for a while longer, eventually resigning themselves to the inevitability of her argument.

Olivia breathed a sigh of relief. She now had the buy in she'd so desperately needed. But it soon became clear that there were other points the team wanted to debate. It was unusual for them to talk together about the way they worked, and they relished the opportunity.

"You know, we could also be more sophisticated in the way we classify types of work," Bea offered. "To get the best from our products, we should sometimes prioritise things other than features, enhancements, and fixes. Occasionally, the next best activity is something completely different—maybe a piece of desk research, a feasibility study, or an experiment—because we simply don't yet know which way to turn."

"That's true!" Charlie chimed in, enthusiastically. "We all know that intuitively, but we don't enshrine those types of work in our backlogs. We just kind of squeeze them in around the edges … and they *feel* squeezed as a result."

"Maybe Digital aren't the only ones who have felt disempowered?" Olivia suggested. "Who here would worry about explicitly adding and estimating those kinds of work, so that they're visible to our stakeholders?"

Everyone looked at everyone else … all at the same time. Quite a feat.

Olivia continued. "But if *we're* the Product Owners, and *we* don't feel empowered to do the right things, no cavalry is coming to save the day. We just do the wrong things. Does that sound okay to anyone here?"

Everyone suddenly felt in urgent need of a trip to the *Coffee Shack*.

No one budged.

Eventually, Charlie laughed. "It's ridiculous, isn't it? No one told us *not* to research or experiment. We're not disempowered at all. The job role we share is probably one of the clearest in Ridgemoor. Let's just empower ourselves, right here and now, to get on and do whatever the hell we want to, so long as we believe it's right."

"… within the rules and policies of the university, of course," Bea added.

"… and maybe the law too!" Olivia clarified, mostly for Charlie's benefit.

"Fair enough!" Charlie accepted, his grin betraying only minor disappointment.

It seemed settled.

"Can I raise something else?" Bea asked.

"Well, *that* didn't sound very empowered!"

The team all laughed at Charlie's joke, pleased to have a moment's respite from today's unusually abstract discussion.

Bea continued. "Tell me if I'm wrong—obviously, I'm the newbie. But there are a couple of external factors acting against us here. First, the Finance team. I don't think they'll smile upon research, feasibility studies, and experiments that further delay the point at which costs can be capitalised."

"You might be right," Olivia noted, furrowing her brow. "Good timing though. I know Vanessa is in a related discussion with Penny already. I'll try to get us into the room, yes?"

Everyone nodded their thanks, hoping for the best.

"And secondly, our annual appraisal objectives don't reward us for keeping our products healthy next year … or the year after. We're incentivised only to bring short-term benefits. So how should we act? Do we do the right thing anyway and risk lower scores? I'm pretty sure Ridgemoor isn't about to sell out to a venture capital firm, so presumably we should care about the long term too?"

Olivia stared at Bea. Another excellent point. Even though her peers were basically good citizens, it couldn't help that the appraisal system rewarded only short term success. Unchanged, it could lead some Product Owners to think *only* about the short term—especially any who planned a change of role in the near future. With luck, others would take the higher ground anyway, either through simple altruism or because they expected to be around later to clear up any mess they created now.

"You're right! We should try to change that," she proposed. "But I'm not sure how. I guess we should be incentivised to meet medium- and long-term product goals, not just short-term success."

"Sounds like the Tragedy of the Commons!" Abhi observed. "When we each focus on what most helps us now, we harm the collective good later on."

"Hmmm. Yes, kind of," Olivia stalled, dredging her long-term memory for the details. Then, recalling, she added, "You know what, I once read that there are three ways to fix that. Let me think … maybe it was education, privatisation or regulation. Feels like our situation might need more than one of those!"

"From what you've told us, we're making progress with some of those already," Bea noted.

Everyone looked at her quizzically.

"You know? We're sitting here now talking about it, prompted by a growing awareness that Digital can see technology debt that we can't. Maybe we need to educate ourselves with more of these conversations, and invite Digital into them too."

Olivia nodded, urging Bea to continue.

"And we're privatising the problem—if I understand the word properly—by ensuring that we each manage our own messes within the boundaries of our products," she added.

"That's true," Olivia confirmed, encouraged. "But we also share some technology platforms, and we look to Digital to manage those. I think we need to indulge Digital's instinct to look after them properly, given that we can't offer much individual ownership there. I guess that's where the ten percent tax comes in."

"I think so," Bea replied. "And finally, there's regulation. I know I've not been here long, but isn't that what the architects do? They should set limits on the technology debt we tolerate … so long as we let them. Maybe that's also part of Digital starting to *do the things right?*"

Olivia stared at Bea, satisfied that Roidgemoor had made an excellent choice in hiring her. She would doubtless be a force for good as the team tackled the remainder of their stalled transformation.

"Maybe we need a Product Owner for incentives! How about you, Bea?" Charlie joked, to mixed reviews.

The meeting over, Olivia reflected on her progress.

She'd won compelling support for Vanessa's plan and looked forward to sharing that news.

She'd try to join Vanessa in discussing funding with Penny.

And she felt confident she could work with Bea and the others to propose a more sustainable incentive scheme.

All in all, a great discussion that would help them move forward convincingly.

Back at base, Vanessa was using every means at her disposal to track Harri down. She was fully briefed now on his discussion with Sukhi, so keen to reach him before tomorrow's meeting with Carla.

Two emails had failed, as had the phone, and he hadn't been at his desk when she stopped by earlier.

Finally, at the end of the day, he returned her call, and described the situation as he saw it.

"Well, thanks for explaining," she responded. "But let me ask you this—would you cap an astronaut's pay just because she didn't have managerial responsibilities? This change seems really old-school. For *years,* we've known and accepted that some technology roles simply command higher salaries. It's demand and supply. We either pay them and hire good staff, or we underpay and get people we could just as well do without. In Digital, one really good developer is probably better than five bad ones. If we want to keep delivering, I don't see any alternative but to pay."

"Carla seems to have a Plan B," he reminded her.

This was infuriating.

"Harri, if we outsource the work, offshore, we can get much cheaper developer days, yes, But, counterintuitively, the outcomes still suffer dramatically. Just think about *Accommod8*."

He tried to interrupt, but she was in full flow.

"And if we outsource *onshore*, we're paying those higher salaries I mentioned anyway, indirectly, plus a profit margin! Most likely, we also lose the right to screen the individuals doing the work, so if the supplier sees more profit in putting the best people on another account, then that's exactly what will happen."

"So, how about using contractors?" Harri proposed.

"You know as well as I do that they're even *more* expensive!" Vanessa protested. "Besides, we're trying to build steady teams with good knowledge of the products and strong relationships inside and outside Digital. A revolving door delivering a succession of contingent labourers won't help us achieve that."

"Well, I understand your points," Harri retorted. "But what we're doing right now hasn't been going great guns either, has it? Let me talk to Carla on your behalf and see what she says. This policy change began in her office."

Vanessa said nothing, but silently modified her notes for her next one-on-one with Carla, due to take place tomorrow. She felt that all the good work she and Olivia had been doing was under unreasonable threat. She'd try to sense how seriously Carla was considering outsourcing Digital, poised ready to consider her own position if needed.

Tuesday's main messages

✓ *Architecture can be thought of simply as that which is difficult to change. Less of it is better.*

✓ *Product owners should focus on 'doing the right things' while Digital concentrates on 'doing the things right'.*

✓ *Digital will see the accumulation of technology debt long before the product owner does, so should raise the issue responsibly.*

✓ *Left untreated, technology debt will reach a critical mass, making payback urgent, and severely limiting product choice for a period.*

✓ *The most effective product backlog contains all significant work in the near term, not just a list of forthcoming features.*

✓ *It's best to incentivise long-term product good, in the form of stable business goals rather than volatile contributory features.*

✓ *Agile thrives on steady staffing and mature relationships, so use payrolled staff in preference to a succession of short-term contractors.*

Wednesday

"Sorry I've only got fifteen minutes today," Carla reminded Vanessa. "Unavoidable, I'm afraid. So let's keep it snappy."

Vanessa had slept fitfully the previous night and was just coming to—despite the two double espressos she'd swigged before cycling in.

"In any case, Penny spoke to me yesterday," Carla acknowledged. "So I can guess what's on *your* agenda. But before we get to that, can you give me the highlights? Are you making headway?"

"Yes. At least I think so," Vanessa opened, with characteristic caution. "Last time we spoke, I explained that Digital had been failing to despatch its duties with the proper professionalism. Not because the people are poor, but because we somehow damaged accountability in adopting Agile."

Carla nodded. She knew that.

Thirteen minutes remained.

"Well, since then we've been rethinking how we should work. My team is bought in, and based on a brief message from Olivia last night, it seems she has the Product Owners on side too."

"Product *Owners*?" Carla queried. This term was new to her.

"Sorry – should have explained. We want to start referring to Olivia and the team as 'owners' instead of 'managers.' It's actually pretty conventional to do that, but it's important as it emphasises their overall accountability for everything about the product."

"You mean, for everything except the digital parts? Those are still with you?" Carla was keen not to blur boundaries.

"Yes and no," Vanessa replied with what was fast becoming her answer to everything. Carla started to frown, so Vanessa quickly moved to clarify.

"Yes, I own Digital. But let's consider what that really means. What we call 'Digital' is just the arrangement of technologies to create a useful self-service experience, which constitutes some part of the wider product. And I'm sure neither of us want both me and Olivia to own *Syllabize*—to pick just one example. So what we've agreed is that Olivia owns the product—the intended experiences and their value, the features that enable them, and the prioritisation of work—but I, or rather the guys in Digital themselves, own the expert production and maintenance of its components."

"Okay," Carla paused, trying to work out what she didn't like. "Not a million miles from what we discussed last time then."

They had ten minutes left.

"So what do *you* do?" she pushed.

Having worked in Manhattan for three years, surrounded by investment bankers and management consultants, Carla was nothing if not direct. Fortunately, Vanessa had known her for just long enough to see through the apparent hostility. And in any case, Vanessa had expected this question.

"I enable. But I have the rest of IT to run too, so it's more accurate to say that I help *Sukhi* to enable."

Carla opened her mouth to ask a question, but was beaten to it.

"What does 'enable' mean?" Vanessa anticipated, quite correctly.

Carla nodded, for once feeling on the back foot herself.

"When we throw together a bunch of marketeers and engineers, it doesn't just *work*. In fact, it would be hard to imagine a better context for personality clashes. But if we get the conditions right, everyone will flourish. That's where my role comes in. I have to build and sustain a culture, team and tools that work well, whatever today's users need. And the teams need to learn to self-improve, too, otherwise, I become a bottleneck. A lot of what they need—and need to do—is pretty clear in their heads anyway, but I flush it out, sense check, and make sure it happens."

Vanessa suppressed a slight smile. She felt she'd pitched her explanation at the right level for her Vice Chancellor.

But Carla was far from satisfied. "So why haven't you?" she asked, slowly and seriously.

Vanessa looked blank. This wasn't the response she'd expected.

"I …," was as far as she got.

"I mean, why haven't you got the conditions right?" Carla persisted.

There had been no need to clarify the question. All Vanessa could think was 'Why haven't *you*, Carla? It's your university!' But this was hardly a reasonable reaction, and in any case, it was Vanessa's university, too.

"I missed this," she admitted.

Then, thinking carefully about what she stood for, and how to express it, she went further.

"I failed. I'm sorry."

It was a strategic risk. Many organisational leaders couldn't be seen to tolerate explicit failure. But Vanessa wasn't sure she wanted to work for one of those people. In her mind, failure was human, and the important thing was to *use* it. Without acknowledging one's own part in a problem, little is learned, so the same mistakes tend to be repeated.

Meanwhile, Carla was privately impressed and encouraged. As luck would have it, she also valued admissions of failure. They were much easier to handle than persistent proclamations of nebulous success. People learn from failure. She'd always felt she could delegate more to people who were honest about their failings so long as they were also keen to develop themselves.

Their backgrounds and experiences differed greatly, but something fundamental connected the two women—a willingness to step outside themselves, analyse their actions, and encourage others to do the same. Suddenly, Carla felt far less enthusiastic about her semi-automatic instinct to outsource Digital. It seemed counterintuitive, but Vanessa's admission of guilt had inculcated far more trust from her boss. Still, Carla couldn't act on gut feeling alone. She needed to test Vanessa a little further.

"Not great," Carla passed judgment on Vanessa's omission. "So, how do I know you'd get it right next time? At least if we outsource, we should be able to assume expert management."

Trying to ignore the slight, Vanessa fingered the printed spreadsheets in her jacket pocket. With the numbers she'd received from her financial controller, and Olivia's annotations, she could objectively oppose outsourcing. Her views would remain arguable but would at least be well-evidenced.

She looked Carla in the eye, as though challenging her to persist with this line. But Carla simply met her gaze and held it.

Vanessa sighed. She released her grip on her pocketed papers, leaving them hidden. Trust, rather than outsourcing, was the real theme of this conversation.

Six minutes remained.

"I can't prove to you now that I'll get this right," she began. "But I believe I will. Here's why …"

Vanessa quickly summarised what she and her team had learned in recent weeks, and the conclusions they'd drawn. She emphasised the closer working relationship with the Product Owners, the standards they expected to embed in the 'definition of done,' their reformed approach to architecture, and their overhauled reporting system.

She explained that the ways of working she'd agreed with Olivia relied on recruiting and retaining smart, right-minded developers, so asked for a let on Harri's salary caps.

Finally, she reminded Carla of some potential downsides of outsourcing, onshore or offshore, as she'd previously done with Penny and Harri. She urged Carla to seek soundings on the outsourcing of *Accommod8* (without revealing that much of the relevant data was concealed in her jacket pocket).

One minute remained. Vanessa had timed her oratory well. It was Carla's turn to talk.

"I appreciate your honesty and openness. Let me be open too—I've already spoken to the Product Owners, and they seem almost as enthusiastic as you are. Good to see that consistency. Moreover, they're your main stakeholders. So if they're happy, then I'm much happier."

Vanessa allowed herself a small smile. But Carla hadn't finished.

"Six weeks. So long as there are no major glitches, we'll take outsourcing off the table then. Is that enough time to show me tangible improvement?"

Vanessa hoped so, and knowing how impatient Carla could be, she didn't feel comfortable asking for longer. She nodded.

"And yes, I'll get Harri off your back. We won't apply the non-management salary caps yet—at least not in Digital. I'll call Harri later today."

The threat was far from over, but Carla's apparent vote of confidence at least gave Vanessa more time. She mustn't falter now. Six weeks would pass quickly.

Wandering over to the *Coffee Shack* for her mid-morning fix, she realised that the experiences of the last two weeks had changed her feelings about her job and about herself. Studying and improving the way that her teams worked was so much more fulfilling than the regular rhythm of status meetings, approvals, and one-on-ones. She felt more interested, energised, and valuable than she had for a long time.

This positive feeling hung in the air for all of thirty seconds or so, just until—rounding a corner—she literally bumped into Penny.

Actually, it was more accurate to say that she bumped into Penny's newly acquired oat milk latte, which promptly tipped itself all over its owner.

Still more accurately, the latte tipped itself into Penny's half-open laptop bag.

Vanessa gasped, in shock.

Penny made a small squeaking noise.

Vanessa fussed around trying to retrieve stray tissues from their various hiding places about her person.

Meanwhile, Penny poured the bag out onto the pavement, to rid herself of the now unwanted latte, but in doing so inadvertently also ridded herself of her purse, keys … and laptop.

Vanessa lurched to grab the laptop, succeeding only in accelerating its short trip towards the ground.

Penny made her small squeaking noise again at the sight of the three *partial* laptops she now owned. (Even for a Finance Director there are occasions when less is more.)

Vanessa apologised profusely, though the responsibility was clearly a shared one.

Penny took a deep breath before speaking.

"It's about time someone installed convex mirrors on these corners! Well, at least I have friends in high places in IT. I expect I can get a replacement quickly?"

Thank goodness Penny had a sense of humour.

Vanessa insisted on replacing the lost latte, so Penny agreed to backtrack to the *Coffee Shack*. The replacement laptop would have to come later. They took a table, and Penny started straightening out her things while they chatted.

"So, we made some headway with that capitalisation question you posed," Penny explained. "Actually, it's a pretty complicated area, and some interpretation is needed. But the gist is that we *should* capitalise the costs of software products, but only once a set of criteria are met. For example, related income should be probable, adequate resources should be available, contributing costs should be clear, and products or features should be well specified or feasibility-tested beforehand."

"Thanks!" Vanessa replied. "That's interesting. Sounds like this is worth exploring in more depth. Since we moved to Agile, some of those criteria aren't met until very late in development. And, of course, we might also develop things that never get released at all—for example if they don't prove technically feasible, or if priorities change. Can I ask why we've tended to capitalise so much in the past?"

"Partly just our interpretation of the standards. But there can be tax advantages to capitalising, and of course lower operational expenditure improves the P&L."

"But doesn't the capital amortisation show on the P&L, as an outgoing?" Vanessa asked, intrigued.

"Yes," Penny admitted. "But only as part of the EBITDA, not the EBIT. And, of course, it's spread over several years. A development expense of say, half a million, in one year looks a lot heavier than an amortisation of £100,000 per year for five years."

"Okay," Vanessa thought she understood. Then she realised the flaw in the logic. "But we're making multiple changes every year, and the intent is that we always will. So even over the medium term, a set of fully amortised development costs will catch up with the equivalent operational expenditure."

"I know there's regular slippage," Penny sought to clarify, "but surely the development projects must end sooner or later?"

"Actually, I don't think so anymore. You see, we don't really run projects. The products need ongoing investment with no set end date. Even though we're changing them, they're being changed … operationally … if you see what I mean?"

"I guess so, yes. And the changes are in small increments, with little or no option to specify well ahead of time?" Again, Penny was keen to clarify.

"That's right. So, are you thinking what I'm thinking?" Vanessa checked.

"Most of the time we needn't capitalise. There's nothing much to gain from it. And in our new world, the standards I mentioned arguably steer us against, rather than towards it."

"Agreed!" Vanessa exclaimed in relief.

But Penny wasn't finished. She paused, deep in thought.

"One more thing. You just mentioned that sometimes Digital develops code that never reaches the users?"

Vanessa's phone rang just as she started to respond. Sukhi was trying to reach her. She declined, keen to hear more from Penny, and confident that they would try again in an emergency.

"Yes. What Sukhi does is pretty complex. So when we start work we're not always certain what the users will value or whether we can develop it. Assuming we *can*, we often won't be sure of the cost at first—so it may or may not be viable to continue."

"Hence the idea of incrementing, to firm those things up, yes?" Penny checked.

"Exactly. If we had stayed with waterfall delivery, with one long-running release, we'd only find out towards the end if it would really work well."

"By which point we've spent most of the money, perhaps to no end?"

Penny sounded like she was seeking clarification, but she understood. She continued.

"So from a financial perspective, where this uncertainty exists, your proposed approach sounds eminently sensible," she conceded.

"I think so," Vanessa confirmed. "We don't like to see time or energy wasted. But that time and energy translates pretty directly into avoidable cost too."

"I'm sorry I didn't trigger this conversation months ago!"

"I'm still sorry about your first latte ... and your laptop!"

They both smiled.

"Don't worry," Penny advised. "If we can systematically avoid wasted cost it will pay for itself in no time!"

As they parted, Penny agreed to work on a reformed funding approach for Digital, with a much lower use of capital. Vanessa thanked her and explained that she'd support her in any way she could. In the meantime, she would brief Sukhi and the others on progress. She headed back to her office, delighted with the outcome of the conversation but just a little concerned about the rate of incoming emails she could see on her phone.

Most of the emails turned out to be predictable, and rather mundane. But she was pleased to see a short memo from Sukhi.

```
From: Sukhi
To: Vanessa
Subject: Backfill for Tim

Hi Vanessa,

I couldn't reach you by phone, but it's easy to
explain by email.

First, Harri has backed off on the non-management
salary caps. Something you did? If so, thanks!

But now he wants to make the role home based, given
the desk space constraints. I don't agree. I know
how  useful  face  to  face  communication  is.
Occasional  home  working  is  fine,  but  this  role
should be office based. Agreed?

Thanks,

Sukhi.
```

```
P.S. Harri also wants me to add a lot more detail
into the job specification. Red tape, but I can do
it.
```

Great that Sukhi had engaged with the problem, appreciated the importance of the issue, and already decided on the best course of action. She wasn't sure all that would have happened even a week ago.

But she wondered if she had spotted a second snag, so rattled off a brief reply.

```
From: Vanessa
To: Sukhi
Subject: Re: Backfill for Tim

Thanks for checking. I think you're spot on! We
want work-life balance, but with the clear intent
that our product teams share a physical space most
of the time.

Incidentally, are you comfortable with Harri's
request to make the role more specific? Aside from
the admin, don't we need people to be flexible —
willing to learn to do things outside a nailed down
job specification — if that's what the backlog
demands? We've seen that when we overspecialise we
tend to create queues everywhere, with everyone
waiting for someone else to do something!

Regards,

Vanessa
```

She'd framed it as a question but felt she knew the answer. No surprise then that half an hour later Sukhi replied, thanking her for spotting the problem, and clearly fired up to defend their shared position.

After the conversation Carla had clearly had with Harri, Vanessa felt that Sukhi would prevail. She wouldn't intervene unless called on, because she wanted to model the delegation of decisions to the people closest to the work. This was something she hoped that Sukhi would pick up on, and reproduce right across Digital.

Wednesday's main messages

✓ *A willingness to fail and learn is as important for an Agile leader as for a developer, and leading by example means seizing opportunities to model that behaviour.*

✓ *Admissions of failure are welcomed by enlightened chiefs, often bringing more responsibility rather than less.*

✓ *The automatic capitalisation of digital development should be challenged, especially where it limits flexibility.*

✓ *Tight job specifications run counter to Agile, tending to introduce more dependencies on outside teams, and thus more delays.*

✓ *Colocation is the best way to enable the kind of rich, regular communication that Agile needs, but virtual colocation can be enabled if needed, using tools like always-on video walls.*

✓ *If colocation isn't possible right now, at least ensure contemporaneity, by closing any significant timezone gaps separating close colleagues.*

Thursday

It had been stormy overnight and was still spitting the next morning. Although the residual water level was now receding the streets stubbornly stayed peppered with perilous puddles.

Early in her cycle ride to work, Vanessa narrowly avoided aquaplaning as she rounded a street corner, so decided to take the rest of the journey more cautiously. She was aware that her phone was persistently piping a panoply of beeps and whistles as she peddled, but sensibly chose to concentrate on the ride.

Dismounting on arrival at Ridgemoor, she was conscious of being soggier than she would prefer at the start of a day's work, but shrugged off the discomfort and checked her phone while walking across to the office.

Disaster.

Based on what she saw in her inbox, she predicted similar stormy weather *inside* the university. For reasons unknown, the *Curricul8* app was suddenly presenting inaccurate timetable information to hundreds of students and their lecturers.

Upping her walking pace now, she kept reading. The only other substantive facts she could garner were that the app had been updated overnight and that the bulk of the new development had been done by a now-departed contingent worker hired by Sukhi to plug a recent capacity gap. So far today, no one had been able to reach that contractor, and a quick scan of his recent social media posts suggested he was now off-grid, deep in the Bolivian jungle.

Her thoughts leapt to how Carla might react. She assumed that the news would reach the Vice Chancellor soon.

Whatever the reaction, Vanessa was determined not to respond defensively. Just like any other kind of failure, occasional bugs were to be expected—perhaps even welcomed—if they helped Digital to learn and ultimately strengthen the products. Besides, fault-free software was almost unheard of, and any that she *had* encountered had been developed at inordinate cost, far surpassing the related benefits.

Nonetheless, the timing was terribly unfortunate. Now more than ever, Vanessa needed to demonstrate Digital's credibility, but her recent reforms wouldn't improve the team's prospects of resolving this incident quickly.

She made her way to her office. It was just before eight thirty, but Sukhi was already hovering outside.

Calm. She'd remain completely calm.

"How are you?" she offered, cheerfully. "I saw the emails, but don't have the full picture yet. Could you brief me … over coffee maybe?"

They headed to the *Shack*, talking as they walked. Sukhi was clearly agitated.

"I'm afraid I don't have the full picture either," they confessed. "The *Curricul8* update was coded by a temp, and we can't reach him now. Unfortunately, he didn't work with anyone else on this, and it looks like he didn't comment the code either, or write specs for the changes he made."

Vanessa was mentally logging all these points. It felt like there were a few more improvements they could make to Digital's working practices. But they could come later.

"Okay," she replied. "But you've got someone on the diagnosis?"

Sukhi hesitated.

"Just me so far."

Vanessa tilted her head a little, trying to elicit a fuller reply. It had worked wonderfully well when Yogi tried it on her, from his vantage point on the nearby bath mat.

Sukhi got the message. Recently they'd been in regular discussions about effective delegation.

"... for now anyway. When the other guys get in, I'll delegate it. Probably to Jack."

"Great. I know you're brilliant at this stuff, Sukhi, but we need other people to grow, and we need you thinking about the problem more broadly please."

Sukhi nodded taking the mild rebuke in the positive spirit in which it was intended.

"So, what exactly are the users seeing?" Vanessa continued.

"A caramel macchiato and a double espresso," Sukhi replied unexpectedly, before turning back to Vanessa to offer a slightly saner response. "The app works fine ... in a sense. All the user interfaces work as intended, it's just that the *data* is wrong for some people. We don't know why yet."

"So, could we at least prevent the wrong data being seen? Temporarily block access to it with a banner maybe?" Vanessa suggested. "No data is better than bad data."

"Yes, I think we should. It's just that ...," Sukhi began examining their fingernails, nervously.

It worked before, so Vanessa simply tilted her head again. She'd already realised that her suggestion of a banner bordered on micromanagement—the very thing she was trying to help everyone else to get away from. Now she wanted Sukhi to continue under their own steam.

"… we haven't built that feature into *Curricul8*. We never had the time. I mean, back then we weren't applying our new 'definition of done', or reserving capacity. And the Product Owner didn't consider scenarios where things go wrong—'unhappy paths' through the user experience. So, right now, the timetable module can only show data. No banners."

This would be difficult to defend to Carla. Vanessa added it to her mental log, and took a deep breath.

"Okay. So we have to work around it another way. I assume Charlie is already on this?" Vanessa was referring to Olivia's peer, the *Curricul8* Product Owner.

Sukhi fidgeted.

Vanessa tilted her head a third time. She must remember to add this technique to her list of favourite management mannerisms, crediting Yogi.

Eventually, Sukhi responded.

"I suppose we were waiting for him to call us."

Vanessa didn't want to condemn her Head of Development. The working day hadn't begun yet, and Sukhi was already deep into the analysis. She paused, and Sukhi filled the gap.

"Yes, okay," they answered the implied question. "We should call Charlie. I'll do that next. I guess he can advise on what kinds of workarounds he'd prefer, while Jack concentrates on the diagnosis."

Coffee in hand now, Sukhi headed back to the labs to get those activities underway.

"You're *seriously* defending all this?" Carla challenged, astonished.

After hearing the news from Sukhi, and offering some initial direction, Charlie had briefed Olivia on the *Curricul8* bug. Like Vanessa, the Product Owners were acutely aware that Carla's reaction to the fault could frustrate their reforms, so together they'd headed straight to her office to lobby for their cause.

"In the last few weeks, I've come to understand Digital much better," Olivia explained. "So now, instead of seeing them as a black box—an appliance—that doesn't do what it's supposed to, I see a smart, knowledgeable, well-motivated team, whose main flaw has been the set of presumptions and received wisdoms they've applied to their work. And I guess you could say that of *our* team too. Not a match made in heaven. But now, through the constructive conversations Vanessa brokered, we've arrived at a promising way forward. Yes, I believe we can turn the situation around quickly."

Carla turned to Charlie.

"And do you feel the same way, given what's happened to *Curricul8*?"

"Not exactly, no," he admitted. "I'm not quite there yet. I don't *disagree*, but I haven't had the same exposure to the inner workings of Digital. Still, I've got huge confidence in Olivia, and what she says makes sense to me."

He paused before continuing. His interactions with Carla had been few and far between, so his brain was whirring as he struggled to read her reaction.

"Besides, I don't know of any sensible alternative. I've worked with Digital products for years, and some of the normal knee-jerk reactions—you know, outsourcing, offshoring, reverting to waterfall methods—just don't seem to work. I'd far rather finish the stalled transformation."

Carla bristled at the mention of outsourcing, before quickly recomposing herself. Had someone mentioned that possibility to Charlie? It was supposed to be highly confidential, for obvious reasons.

"Maybe the timing is helpful ... in a perverse way," Carla thought aloud. "It brings this thing to a head. If Digital can fix the fault quickly and professionally, then that result—combined with your belief—would tend to support the view that there's been positive progress."

Olivia nodded, but had heard the "if," and feared what was coming.

"But if *not*, we need to make some changes around here … knee-jerk or otherwise!" Carla continued, her uncomfortable gaze now panning across to Charlie. "Look, I'm running late. But I appreciate your openness, and your willingness to take a controversial position. I'll need regular updates until *Curricul8* is fixed."

"Will do," Charlie agreed, and the two Product Owners headed back to the labs.

Thursday's main messages

✓ *Live bugs are bad news, but they're inevitable from time-to-time, and are an excellent stimulus for systemic improvement.*

✓ *However robust your product appears to be, it's wise to design for a range of 'failure cases'.*

✓ *Documentation is deceptively important, forcing more rigorous thinking in design and development, assisting cross-skilling, improving security, and accelerating maintenance and support.*

Friday

By Friday morning, the storms had cleared, and the sun shone happily on the umbrella-capped tables outside ¡Coman Eat!—Ridgemoor's popular tapas bar.

Pedro eyed it suspiciously on his approach. It wasn't popular with *him*. Had the sushi restaurant been open in the morning, he would certainly have preferred that they meet there instead to further their discussions on Digital.

Aisha and Colin were already ensconced, and examining the extensive menu. In a bid to accommodate the bar's less adventurous clientele, it covered British basics as well as Spanish tapas.

Pedro selected a seat between the others, tipped his chair to remove its residual rainfall, and gingerly sat down. He greeted them briefly, then joined them in giving his full attention to the menu. Ten pages of tapas seemed too much, especially at breakfast time, and every so often his brow would knit, or his eyes roll, as he scanned its pages suspiciously.

Eventually, the three colleagues began to make their choices. Colin was the first to lower his menu. He didn't seem to notice that the others were still stuck in silent study.

"So after last time we met, I had a few ideas," he opened proudly. His chest was inflated now, and he was leaning forward on the table awaiting an invitation to elaborate.

His interjection briefly interrupted the others' menu musings, but they battled on bravely.

Colin didn't always get the cues he hoped for, but had learned not to let that slow him down. After waiting a few seconds, he decided that he should elaborate regardless.

"I've decided to help fix Digital. I'm going to deploy three of my team to Sukhi," he explained.

The others didn't want to risk a misunderstanding, so lowered their menus momentarily in unison to check they were hearing this right.

Pedro led the way. "You will give three people to Sukhi?"

"Yes … well, *lend*. I'd want them back eventually. But in the meantime, they could work on standardising and automating the

Digital infrastructure and operational tools. I think it's the right thing to do," he said proudly.

"Good idea!" Pedro volunteered generously, distinctly recalling that this had been his own idea in the first place. "But, what are their skills?"

"Pretty strong. Between them, they've created DevOps pipelines, automated SecOps, and created a self-service cloud catalogue for Digital. They're actually very keen to reuse those skills here."

"And who would manage them while they are working on Digital?" Aisha asked.

"Well, Sukhi could. But I'd have a watching brief, too."

Pedro and Aisha suspected that Colin's change of heart was self interested, at least in part. Perhaps he wanted to learn more about newer technologies and tools, or just win more recognition for his part in the reforms.

"This is very helpful," Pedro reaffirmed. "What a good idea! I hope Sukhi agrees. I guess we just need to be clear on what a 'watching brief' is. Maybe we could use the same *Why-What-When vs. How-Who-Where* model that Sukhi and the Product Owners are using?"

"Yes!" said Aisha, thinking quickly. "But now with Sukhi in the other seat."

The others looked at her blankly.

"You know," she continued. "We should set Sukhi up as a kind of 'Product Owner' for Digital infrastructure and operations, and Colin's guys can be the product developers. Sukhi decides *what* they need, *why* and *when*, expressing it in a backlog, and the loaned staff make the improvements accordingly. But they decide, with Colin, *how* to make those improvements. We treat the Digital labs like a product in their own right."

Pedro looked proud, Colin alarmed. Both could immediately see how naturally the same divide of responsibilities could apply again here, but that certainly wasn't what Colin had intended. He'd expected to leave himself many more levers. Nonetheless, the logic was irresistible, so the offer to Sukhi seemed settled.

"Good idea, Colin!" Aisha concluded, just as a waiter arrived to take their orders.

Meanwhile, across campus, Sukhi, Jack, and their teams were still hard at work on *Curricul8*. Charlie had joined them, and was anxious to steer and support the work wherever he could.

Only two backlog items were getting any attention today: the diagnosis of the underlying timetable problem, and the introduction of a temporary holding screen to obscure any data which might be invalid.

After a lot of hard work, the latter was now in testing, with the expectation that it could be deployed later that morning.

But the diagnosis was still underway, and still no one had been able to reach the errant developer. The team had spoken to his Mum, but it transpired that her software engineering credentials were woefully limited.

Undaunted in his pursuit of the problem, Jack had intensively examined hundreds of lines of almost impenetrable code. Suddenly now he spotted a problem, sat back in his chair, and lifted both arms in the air triumphantly.

"It's the old database!" he announced, visibly relieved. "When we upgraded the data server six months ago, we left the old database in place, so we could fail back to it if needed. It's out of date, but it's still there—we forgot to drop it—and the recent software upgrade pointed most of the queries back to it. I guess the contractor we used wouldn't have known to override that. For that matter, neither would his Mum."

With near-perfect timing, Vanessa chose just that moment to join them in the labs, keen to show her support. Listening from the sidelines, she quickly caught up with the news.

She and Sukhi congratulated Jack on his hard-won discovery. Then, while Jack turned his attention to the fix, they retired to a nearby meeting room to consider what wider lessons could be learned from the troublesome turn of events.

"I guess you'll examine what happened, and what we can learn from it in the next retrospective?" Vanessa checked.

Sukhi nodded. "Yes, and the developers are more enthusiastic about the retros again now. I think they get the message that it's their meeting, not mine. After we spoke last Friday, I've backed off, giving them more ownership of their ways of working—except where there are cross-team dependencies."

"Great!" Vanessa said approvingly. This was the style of management she wanted to see. Direction setting and enabling, rather than prescribing unnecessarily.

"A couple of things jump out for me so far," Sukhi started. "First, obviously, we failed to tidy up the live environment. We left a derelict database *in situ*, which complicated our diagnosis. We should have remembered to remove it shortly after it fell out of use. And we should get in the habit of doing that kind of housekeeping routinely, without fail. Yet another form of technology debt!"

"Agreed. Good spot," Vanessa chimed in supportively. "Anything else you'd like to change?"

"Yes," Sukhi continued. "I think we've undervalued the importance of documentation. A data architecture or inventory should have exposed the fact that the old database was still present. And there should have been a procedure or script to stop app upgrades reverting to it. I don't like relying on manual steps as they're too easily overlooked."

Vanessa smiled. Another improvement that made sense to her. "The new 'definition of done' should help here, I guess?" she asked.

"Definitely. It requires us to produce documentation. But the new code was written just before we adopted it."

Sukhi paused, looking momentarily troubled.

"You know what, though? We haven't been very clear on *what* documentation we expect or to what level of detail. I'll work with the team to set a standard. Too much documentation could be almost as bad as too little. I don't want the team losing a lot of time writing pages of text that no one uses, or that's too hard to maintain cleanly."

Vanessa was reminded of something she saw in an email the previous morning, while she and her bike were dripping onto the university forecourt. "I think I also read that some of our code isn't well commented?"

"Yes," Sukhi admitted. "We could certainly be a lot better there. But comments are a form of documentation too, so I'll cover them in the standards."

Sukhi reflected for a moment, then continued, "And we didn't manage the temp very well, did we? It's hard to justify running a full induction for temps, especially on the high day rates we pay, but this fault emphasises the risks we run when we don't. I'll try to avoid short term hiring in future, even if it means some slippage."

"Sounds sensible." Vanessa was impressed by both the richness of the conversation and her Head of Development's burgeoning self-assurance. She was used to Sukhi looking like a deer in the headlights when anything went wrong, but now they were fully engaged, calmly hunting down problems, and committing to improvements—without a hint of self-flagellation.

"Oh, and what about the test environments?" Sukhi asked, rhetorically. "We know that they're not exact replicas of production, but I'd expect the vast majority of faults to be spotted there, before there's any real damage done. I'll take a look at that too. Anything else you can think of, Vanessa?"

She was delighted to be invited.

"Maybe a couple of things, but you might have them in hand already. One, 'unhappy path' user stories and testing. Maybe we should routinely plan for failure scenarios and make sure they're trapped gracefully to limit damage." Suddenly remembering something she'd read she added, "Doesn't Netflix do a lot of that?"

Sukhi grinned. "I'm sure most mature Digital operations do. And we should, too. Actually, Netflix supposedly goes much further. They wrote their own gremlin called 'Chaos Monkey' that actually tries to sabotage their own production environment in a variety of inventive ways, so they can strength-test and improve it. Maybe we'll get there … one day … but for now, let's just start handling those 'unhappy paths' gracefully. I'll talk to the Product Owners."

"Sounds good," Vanessa agreed. "My only other thought was about putting all our eggs in one basket. It looks like we only had one person intimate with this piece of code, right?"

"Yes," Sukhi accepted. "Not great, is it? We've looked into 'pair programming' before—where two people work on every code change."

Vanessa raised an eyebrow. That sounded expensive, but she was open-minded.

Sukhi saw her surprise. "It's not as crazy as it sounds. Two heads are often better than one, and it guards against the specific risk that just materialised for us. But we don't get a lot of faults like this. A better next step would be to ensure peer review of all new code before release. Another item for our 'definition of done'!"

"Great," Vanessa returned. "That sounds like a lot to be going on with. It really demonstrates the value we can derive from a fault. I think I just counted six substantial improvements you could adopt. I'll be keen to hear how that goes. Thanks for putting your focus on this, Sukhi. It's exactly what I need. Jack will be competent to fix the fault, but you can create much more value looking at the 'means of production' and how they can be improved … even if you'd sometimes rather be out there coding!" she smiled.

"Actually, this is fun too," Sukhi was forced to admit. "It's just a different type of problem solving. And those six improvements will make far more impact than writing a few lines of code. I'll prompt the teams to feed them into their retrospectives. Thanks for helping out, Vanessa."

They parted company, and Vanessa headed over to the *Shack* to grab a sandwich (and double espresso) for lunch later, pausing only briefly to catch up with Charlie on her way out.

Returning to her desk Vanessa found a brief email from Carla, written in reply to Charlie's latest update. Taking a deep breath, she opened it.

```
From: Carla
To: Charlie
Cc: Vanessa
Subject: Re: Update on Curricul8 fault

Charlie,

That's a helpful update. I don't need to see any
more of these now.

Vanessa, this was a pretty bad bug, but the
remediation was well managed. Let's discuss at our
next meeting on Monday.

Well done both.

Carla.


From: Charlie
To: Carla
Cc: Vanessa
Subject: Update on Curricul8 fault
```

```
Carla,

I've spent the morning in the labs again. Here's
the latest:

-  To   date,   we   think   500-600   students   have
experienced  the  fault,  but  very  few  have  actually
missed lectures.

-  We're  releasing  an  enhancement  now  to  stop
inaccurate data appearing.

- In parallel, Digital just found the cause of the
fault. It should be fixed today.

- We'll build in new controls to stop similar faults
in the future to Curricul8 and other apps.

Charlie.
```

Guarded support from Carla then, but Vanessa wondered how much she could really read into the Vice Chancellor's short response.

She penned her own cautious acknowledgement, also suggesting that she and Carla move the venue for their Monday meeting to the Digital labs. If Carla accepted, she'd be sure to have one of the Product Owners waiting in the wings.

Friday's main messages

✓ *Infrastructure experts can lend valuable skills to digital, benefitting both, as well as the enterprise at large.*

✓ *A failure to tidy-up will likely result in more technology debt, threatening service stability and future change.*

✓ *Automated deployment using infrastructure-as-code can dramatically reduce risky discrepancies between test and production environments.*

Weekend

A fairly private person, Vanessa had said nothing to her colleagues about her recent fortieth birthday. To mark the occasion, her brother had generously paid for a spa day for two, and she and Maddie had used it to book treatments on Sunday. It wasn't Vanessa's *favourite* way to spend a day, but a change was sometimes as good as a rest. She'd throw herself into the experience, and would certainly be intrigued to see what Maddie made of it.

On the drive there, they chatted as normal, reflecting on the previous week's events and the day ahead. Prompted by a recent careers fair at school, Maddie asked her Mum to explain her job at the university.

Vanessa sighed inwardly. She found that *most* technology jobs became boring or unintelligible (or both) as soon as anyone tried to explain them to an outsider. She'd previously tried to use analogies, but to no avail. At times like these, she almost wished she'd opted for a job as a doctor, chef or street sweeper.

"Well," she began shakily. "I'm in charge of Digital and IT for the University. But you already know that?"

"Yes," Maddie agreed. "Though I don't know what 'Digital' actually is. Not really."

"That's fair! It's very ambiguous, actually," Vanessa laughed. "It means slightly different things in different places. But at Ridgemoor, it means all the software that we provide for students to use, especially from their own laptops and phones."

"So nothing to do with digits, then? Just a different way of using IT."

Like her Mum, Maddie was a stickler for specifics.

"More or less, yes," Vanessa was forced to concede.

"So, I get that you're in charge. But what do you actually *do*? And would *I* like doing it?"

Career planning at age thirteen seemed a little precocious to Vanessa, but teenagers seemed to look further ahead than they used to, and she was keen to help if she could. She considered the question carefully, especially given the turn her work had taken of late.

"Well, if you'd asked me last month, I'd probably have said that I organise and plan how we provide useful technology to people at the university, make sure it actually *is* provided, and keep it working as intended."

"Okay. Sounds pretty dull! But what would you say *now*?" Maddie asked doggedly.

"It's been a weird month," her Mum explained. "I'm actually reconsidering my role. Let's just say that—while I still do all those 'dull' things—I now put more time into helping other people to do them, and to working out how to get better and better at it. Unfortunately, improvement doesn't happen automatically in large organisations."

"Still pretty ambiguous, Mum!" Maddie chided. "So, would *I* like it?"

"I don't know, Maddie. I just don't know. But I know that *I* do," she grinned.

Fun fact for the weekend

✓ *At time of writing, NIST defines 'digital' as 'the coding scheme generally used in computer technology to represent data'.*

(No wonder Maddie is confused.)

Week Four

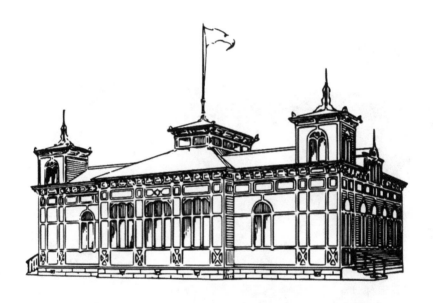

Monday

Two sauna sessions, two pedicures, and one glass of prosecco later, and Monday rolled around again.

The sun streamed in through the lab windows as Vanessa, Olivia, Sukhi and the developers awaited Carla's arrival.

Right on time, she strutted confidently through the swing doors with Penny in tow. Vanessa walked over to greet them while the others hung back chatting amongst themselves.

Vanessa was pretty sure that Carla and Penny wouldn't want to see the Digital team's DevSecOps pipelines in full flow, so she moved them quickly around the room, only drawing attention to the attitude and enthusiasm of the team.

Concluding her short tour, Vanessa asked Carla if Olivia and Sukhi could join their meeting. Carla seemed surprised but had already planned to bring Penny along, so acquiesced quickly enough.

"Actually, it's good that we're all here together," Carla opened as they took their seats in the lab's meeting room. She was always one to exploit a situation to best advantage.

"I've heard some very positive things about Digital in recent weeks, despite last week's disastrous outage. But I have a few outstanding questions."

Vanessa was relieved that she'd had the foresight to bring Olivia and Sukhi along. But Carla's first question was aimed elsewhere.

"First, Penny. Cost. Tell me why the way that Vanessa wants to work will be cheaper than the old method … 'waterfall' … and cheaper than moving the work outside the university."

Sukhi winced involuntarily. Vanessa hadn't mentioned that outsourcing was under consideration.

Penny's response was matter of fact. "It may not always be. Especially in situations where everyone knows precisely what's needed, and how to make it work. But I've come to understand that those two conditions are rarely met in Digital. So, the approach that Vanessa and Olivia are proposing is valuable. It lets us find out early what will be beneficial and what won't, then target our spending accordingly, free from cross-continental communication problems, competing motivations and provider profit margins."

"Okay. Interesting," Carla conceded. "I'll buy it for now, and I guess we'll find out the truth over time. But can you work with Vanessa and Olivia on a model that compares the approaches over the long term?"

Penny nodded, while Carla continued.

"Next. Speed. Maybe this is one for you Olivia, as you're here. How does our pace compare with other ways of delivering Digital?"

Olivia was happy to tackle that one, choosing to do so with reference to Penny's previous answer.

"Actually, it's a similar story," she started.

Did Carla's eyes narrow at the injudicious use of the word 'story'? Olivia pushed on undaunted. Long gone were the days when she might have chastised herself for imperfect phraseology.

"We save time in the same way that we save money—by avoiding wasted effort. You'd be amazed how much of both we used to waste with waterfall. But our time-to-market is faster this way, too, because we don't bundle up features for mass release in a year's time. Instead, we drip-feed improvements through as they're developed. So, some features come into use nearly a year earlier than they otherwise would."

Carla nodded, impressed. Vanessa wasn't sure if she was impressed with Olivia's answer or just with Olivia.

"Yes. I remember the business case. So you still believe in it, two years on?"

"Absolutely!" Olivia asserted. "But we failed to finish the transformation, so haven't reaped all the rewards so far. Vanessa is fixing that now," she offered magnanimously.

"Okay, last one," Carla persisted. "What about quality … especially in light of what happened last week? Vanessa, how does your method compare?"

Vanessa decided to take a risk. She'd spent more time than most adjusting to Carla's idiosyncrasies, but wanted to live out her newly adopted management style, so decided to delegate the answer.

"Sukhi can explain that far better than I can … if that's okay?"

Carla was firm but not vindictive, so nodded her agreement despite her long-held reservations about talking to techies.

Sukhi cleared their throat, remembered how important brevity would be, and explained.

"The quality comparison is more subtle. Waterfall can deliver very high quality, while immature Agile labs can introduce a lot of error—especially when they rush or act carelessly."

Vanessa's heart dropped a little.

Carla remained expressionless.

But Sukhi hadn't finished.

"… but we're not going to do either of those things," they explained, quietly and confidently. "Olivia and the team have enthusiastically accepted our 'definition of done' which ensures that all work completes cleanly, or not at all. Last week's bug was a result of the old regime. There will always be *some* bugs of course, but I expect to get them down below levels comparable with well-managed waterfall, and because of our automation, we can fix them *faster*. The automation also lets us run far more quality checks than ever before. In fact, we're going to start writing the checks before we write the software."

Carla listened intently. Sukhi's explanation was clearer than expected. Dozens of questions sprang to mind, but she had learned that a Vice Chancellor couldn't expect to delve into detail everywhere. Instead, she read the room. Everyone was nodding calmly and confidently.

"Right," she accepted. "Sounds promising."

Vanessa was also very pleased with Sukhi's response, but had something of her own to add.

"There's one more thing, Carla, if I may? The human factor."

Carla leaned forward, wondering where Vanessa was going with this.

"When we create solutions, we work with creative people. They don't do it just for the salary at the end of the month. If we regiment everything around them, plan it to the 'nth' level of detail, then micromanage and measure their activities, we dampen their spirits ... and their creativity. There are hundreds of other places they could work—probably for more money—as we started to see recently. Sukhi and I want to respect and cultivate our Digital team, trusting their professionalism and bringing out the best in each of them. That's why I come to work now."

Carla was taken aback at this assertive stance. She thought that *she* decided the CDIO's role! Nonetheless, Vanessa's outlook was remarkably close to her own. Finally, she responded.

"I don't disagree. And maybe we can use this elsewhere in Ridgemoor?"

Vanessa smiled, answering Carla's question with two of her own.

"How is your chess?" she asked. "And are you free this evening?"

Monday's main messages

✓ *Agile should be faster than waterfall whenever user needs are complex or changeable, but may not be otherwise.*

✓ *Much of the cost efficiency of Agile comes from avoiding work that would have limited value—perhaps because user needs or technology limitations weren't adequately understood or because the product context changed.*

✓ *Another obvious benefit is that some features will launch earlier, giving more time for returns to accrue.*

✓ *Code quality is not inherently better with Agile, but the automation required for rapid iteration offers more opportunities to assure it.*

✓ *In a well-run Agile regime, workers seem to form stronger bonds with colleagues, feel more shared ownership of problems, reduce wasted time and effort, get a regular rush from real-world deployment, can see the impact they're having on the world, and as a result, feel more fulfilled in their jobs.*

✓ *Far from being limited to software development, this way of working can be adopted successfully in most creative environments.*

Epilogue

Carla's six-week deadline is long passed.

No matter. She forgot all about it two months ago. Right now, she's more focused on kicking off culture change right around Ridgemoor.

Olivia stopped to help a fallen runner in the triathlon but somehow still secured the silver. At work, she's been promoted to Chief Product Owner, with reach across all of Ridgemoor's products. Colleagues are pleased that she's genuinely dismissive of the new job title, seeing herself only as 'servant leader' to the rest of the team. She feels little has changed in her day to day work, but now benefits from a little more authority in pioneering new ways of working. With outside expertise, she's honing Ridgemoor's incentives to reward sustainable product ownership, reducing the accumulation of technology debt.

Penny is enjoying life. A person of highbrow habits, she's picked up a passion for the piano—and especially Bach's Goldberg Variations. Never short of energy, she's also started collaborating with an analyst firm on a whitepaper entitled 'Accounting for Agile'—a topic she still finds intriguing. Everyone sees her as supremely wise … but then, they always did.

Harri is in a very different place. Two weeks ago, Carla explained to him why he no longer wanted to work at Ridgemoor. He felt obliged to agree.

Aisha has developed greater pragmatism and acceptance, making peace with the wider world. Despite its critical importance, she's learned that IT security won't always come ahead of everything else. Her Zen meditation classes have been invaluable in helping her come to terms with this reality.

Colin is still supportive of the digital reforms. But he's still Colin, too. In his mind he's been promoted to become Vanessa's deputy. In reality, he hasn't.

Pedro has signed up for an evening class on Spanish cuisine. He never really overcame his discomfort with breakfasting at *¡Coman Eat!* and now wants to hone his culinary skills. His Spanish heritage means he's implicitly seen as the star pupil there. Meanwhile, at Tuesday's SLT meetings, he is implicitly seen as Vanessa's deputy.

Sukhi just sponsored Olivia for next year's triathlon. They chat almost every day and sometimes meet up at weekends.

Sukhi has also started using student developers. It works well. They benefit from real-world work experience as part of their computing, marketing or product design degrees, they're available outside term time when the other developers tend to take vacation, and they stick around for much longer than two weeks.

The last few months have reinvigorated Miles in his role. He's consulted widely on how to add the most value and realised that the answer was in the question. Value itself will be his watchword, and with Vanessa's agreement he's transforming his own team into a *Value Management Office* spanning all of delivery.

A family of pigeons have moved into Yogi's favourite tree. Much like Miles, he feels reinvigorated.

Maddie is bemused by Yogi's new obsession, and even more bemused when she wins the Monday night chess league. (She had no idea she was so good.) And she's still bemused by her Mum's job, of course. But she's nearly fourteen now, so far more concerned with proper teenage matters.

Naturally, Vanessa has been offered a larger role. Given her aptitude for driving improvement, she's spearheading internal transformation for Carla right around the University. It's challenging, but she's never enjoyed anything more. She remains CDIO, too, but is confident in delegating to her sharp, engaged SLT.

She just missed an impromptu call from Tim and wonders if his new job is working out as well as he'd hoped.

Then there's Casey.

After they met at chess club, Carla offered him a part-time, salaried role as advisor to her and Vanessa.

He took the role, but not the salary.

No one knows why.

Vanessa hasn't asked.

To her, it seemed like one question too many.

Afterword

The short novel you just read concerns itself with the virtues of shifting to a coherent set of working practices, which is nonetheless radically different from traditional delivery management. A set that we've inadvertently inhibited by industrialising change over decades—especially with formal project and programme management.

I believe that the shift is of huge societal importance because, as well as being more effective and efficient in many organisational contexts, it's also more *fulfilling* for any professionals responsible for making or improving anything. It changes the nature of work.

It's largely based on Agile thinking, though I avoided using that word as much as possible in the narrative because it scarcely seems to capture the magnitude of the opportunity on offer. Besides, I also include elements of complementary thinking from Lean, Design Thinking and DevOps (terms that I avoided much more successfully).

I intended the many conversations in the book to represent those that are actually needed to effect meaningful change of this type at a typical large organisation. But I admit that I cheated a little. I used characters who were, on the whole, fairly amenable to change. This is the main reason that Vanessa and her colleagues seemed to shift so far in just three weeks. Expect any equivalent transformation in your organisation to take longer.

Did I also cheat by granting Ridgemoor a partial transformation at the start of the story? No, I don't think so. Most organisations have already begun thinking differently, but become stuck, just like Ridgemoor. They've shifted one set of conventions for another, which is unlikely to match their original intent. Their troubled transformations may or may not have brought net improvements. I would urge them to continue, conditions permitting.

It's worth noting that the ideas in this book can be applied successfully far beyond Digital and IT. If you do decide to borrow any of them, my only additional counsel would be as follows: ensure adequate enlightened leadership is in place, focus on the way that staff *feel* in their roles, and keep everything as overtly simple and sensible as it can possibly be.

In the meantime, I'd welcome any questions, comments or suggestions by email to jeremy@ridgemoor.uk.

Good luck!

Bibliography

None of the publications listed below have been cited specifically in this book, but they have been the most significant in helping me to form the ideas it embodies, so are recommended reading for anyone interested in deepening their understanding. They are listed in order of author surname.

The Agile Architecture Revolution, Jason Bloomberg

The Six Enablers of Business Agility, Karim Harbott

The DevOps Handbook, Gene Kim et al.

Large Scale Scrum, Craig Larman & Bas Vodde

Turn the Ship Around, L. David Marquet

Thinking in Systems, Donella H. Meadows

The Culture Map, Erin Meyer

Agile Product Ownership, Roman Pichler

Chess and the Art of EA, Gerben Wierda

Extreme Ownership, Jocko Willink & Leif Babin

Acknowledgements

Thanks are due to a few people who have influenced the content of this book, or supported me in writing it.

My wonderful wife Sarah, who encouraged me to put pen to paper, reviewed the first full draft, and remained philosophical when she learned that her least favourite chapter was my favourite.

My marvellous daughter Bea, who lent her name (and some of her personality traits) to one of the characters.

Senior managers at Mason Advisory, my current employer, who enthusiastically supported publication, even though they may not share every opinion expressed here.

Dave W, for his 'no holds barred' review of the first full draft.

All of 'The Squad' who helped me to understand the less tangible benefits of Agile working, and were happy to share in the costs of the asparagus.

And Lin-Manuel Miranda, for writing *Hamilton*, and thereby helping Vanessa to wind down at the weekend.